Of Beetles and Angels

A True Story of The American Dream

Of Beetles and Angels

A True Story of The American Dream

Mawi Asgedom

Edited by Dave Berger

megadee books

PUBLISHED BY megadee books
P.O. BOX 57060, Chicago, IL 60657-060

Publisher's Cataloging-in-Publication
(Provided by Quality Books, Inc)
Asgedom, Mawi.
    Of beetles and angels: a true story of the American
Dream / author, Mawi Asgedom; editor, Dave Berger –
1st ed.
    p. cm.
Hardcover ISBN: 0-9704982-6-8
Paperback ISBN: 0-9704982-7-6

1. Asgedom, Mawi 2. Success 3. Ethiopians—United
States—Biography 4. Eritreans—United States—Biography
I. Title.

BF637.S8A84 2001   158.1'092
                                          QBI00-818

Cover Design: Richelle Fischer
Author Photo: Patricia "Raven" Moorehouse
Kafka Translation by Nisrin El Amin

Editor: Dave Berger

Attention Schools / Organizations: *Quantity discounts are
available on bulk purchases. For information, please call
630.660.8864 or write to the address above.*

To the true hero of this story, my mother Tsege

Author's Note

Although I have written this book under the name "Mawi Asgedom," my full name is Selamawi Haileab Asgedom. I was given that name by my Aunt Mehret.

When I was a baby, Aunt Mehret escaped heavy warfare in her hometown and came to stay with us. Upon arriving at our home, she told my parents, "You must change your baby's name from 'Elias' to 'Selamawi.' For I have come out of warfare into peace."

"Selam" means "peace;" "Selamawi" means "peaceful."

In this book, several people's names have been changed to protect their anonymity.

I have also taken especially great pains to leave politics out of this book. I pray that my brothers and sisters from Eritrea and Ethiopia will find no bias in my writings, for I love both countries equally.

Selamawi Haileab Asgedom
October 29, 2000
Chicago, Illinois

Table of Contents

Map of Eritrea and Ethiopia

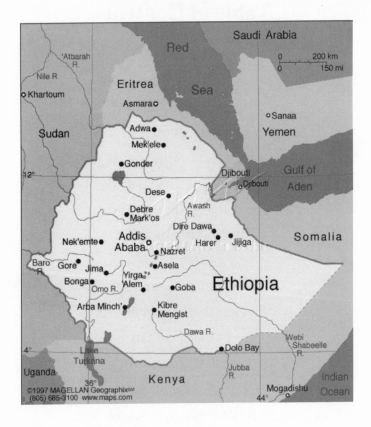

Special thanks to Maps.com for permission to reproduce this map.

Of Beetles and Angels

Memories

The desert, I remember. The shrieking hyenas, I remember. But beyond that, I cannot separate what I remember from what I have heard in stories.

I may or may not remember seeing my mother look at our house in Adi Wahla, Ethiopia, just before we left. Gazing at it as though it were a person whom she loved and cherished. Trance-walking to the house's white exterior, laying her hands on it for a few moments, feeling its heartbeat—feeling her own heartbeat—then kissing it, knowing that she might never see it again.

I remember playing soccer with rocks, and a strange man telling me and my brother Tewolde that we had to go on a trip, and Tewolde refusing to go. The man took out a piece of gum, and Tewolde happily traded his homeland.

I remember our journey and the woman we met. Despite her fatigue, she walked and walked and walked, trying to limp her way to safety across miles of stones and rocks. She continued to limp, wanting to stop, but knowing that if she did, she wouldn't move again.

She pressed on and on, and soon her limp became a crawl. And then I saw a sight that I would never forget—the soles of her naked feet melting away, and then disappearing into the desert, leaving only her bloody, red flesh, mixed with brownish sand and dirt.

But still, she kept on limping. For what choice does a refugee have?

We had no choice, either. We—my mother, my five-year-old brother, my baby sister, and I—kept walking, hoping that we would make it to Sudan and find my father. He had fled our war-ravaged home a year earlier, driven away by the advancing Ethiopian army.

Even stories fail me as I try to recall the rest of our journey. I know only that the wilderness took its toll, that our young bodies gave way, and that we entered a more barren and deadly internal wilderness.

We crossed the Sudanese border and arrived at a city called Awad. A sign should have been posted at the city limits: *Awad, home of the exiled. Home of the hopeless. Home of the diseased.* A simple sign that would warn and welcome us all.

Welcome, all you refugees. All you psychologically tormented. All you physically malnourished. All you uprooted. Rest your burdens here, for you can rest them nowhere else. Rest your hopes here, for no other place will accept them.

But do not hope too much. For too much hope can lead to insanity.

Beware. We can ill treat your ailments. We have few pills here and little life. We have no guarantees that medicine, not flour, fills the pills. But you have no choice, and neither do we. For we give only that which we have.

Beware our fishermen. Where's the water, you ask? There is no water. They fish strangers, vagabonds, foreigners, refugees. They look for you even now; if they find you, they will drag you with their iron nets to a wilderness hell.

Please do not blame us. What would you do if chaos approached you on the tortured feet of a million refugees? Could you handle so many?

I don't remember avoiding the iron nets or finding my father. But I do remember seeking safety in a Sudanese refugee camp. My family spent three years there.

But the camp had its own problems. Disease took its toll, famine always threatened, and warfare plagued Sudan.

Although the fighting never reached our camp, the Sudanese armies were always looking for new soldiers. And they didn't hesitate to draft refugees.

My parents wondered: What kind of future do we have here? What kind of future do our kids have?

They started hearing more and more about a distant land, a paradise where everyone had a future.

And then, one day, they decided that they'd had enough. War at home. War in Sudan. They wanted peace, and they were ready to go. The village elders watched them prepare and offered a few words of wisdom.

Heading to America, are you? They say that everyone there drives big cars and lives in big houses. Money flows through streets of glimmering gold. And everyone lives long, easy lives.

You will undoubtedly be happy there. Go well, live long, and please, do not forget us.

But as you gather your belongings, please permit us a few words of caution. We may be the poorest and least educated of folks, Ethiopian and Eritrean refugees living in Nowhere, Sudan, but even we have heard things that may interest you.

America seems sweet on top, like fresh honey straight from the comb. But what's sweet on the surface is often rotten underneath. So beware.

Beware your skins. Blacks are treated like adgi in America, like packhorses. Beware, too, of thieves. Yes, thieves who steal much more than money—thieves who can loot minds, cultures, and even bodies.

Most of all, please remember your country and remember us. Remember your people.

A New Life

We spent our first two weeks in America in a two-room, two-bed motel room in Chicago, my parents on one bed, and on the other, all of us children. Then we moved for seven weeks to a motel in suburban Wheaton.

Knowing that we could get lost in the maze of streets and homes, we rarely left the motel, unless we were accompanied by World Relief, the organization that had brought my family.

One day, though, my father decided that we should brave the new country on our own. *TEWOLDE AND SELAMAWI, GET YOUR SHOES ON,* he announced. *WE NEED TO LET THE OUTSIDE AIR BEAT ON US.*

Sporting fully-picked afros and sun-broiled, Sudanese skin, clad in mismatched second hand clothes and low-budget Sudanese shoes, we trekked along the shoulder of IL 38. Needless to say, we drew plenty of looks.

We walked until our new shoes tore into the soles of our feet. Night approached, and thousands of headlights, more lights than we had ever seen in our lives, streamed past our eyes.

We watched in wonder, unable to believe that one road could hold so many cars. My father's voice assumed an uncharacteristic hush.

THEY WERE RIGHT, he told us in amazement. *I DON'T KNOW HOW THEY KNEW, BUT THEY WERE RIGHT. NO SMALL CARS HERE. EVERYONE DRIVES BIG CARS. AND NIGHT HAS NO POWER OVER THEM.*

If he could have read his future, my father might have feared the headlights. He might have seen the destructive power behind them, power that would one day take his life. But he could hardly read his new country's language, much less his future, so he remained amazed all the way home.

The other times we left our motel were with our World Relief friends. They came almost daily and took us around Chicago—to parks, to skyscrapers, to the grocery store, showing us what life would be like in America.

Even with their constant support, though, we still felt the deepest homesickness. We yearned for a piece of *injera* bread or a bowl of *sebhi* stew. For a neighbor who spoke our language. For our people.

That's when they appeared. Out of nowhere, two angels at our door. It was two of our people: *habesha* women. And they came bearing gifts: *injera* bread and *sebhi* stew.

My mother burst into tears upon seeing them. *"How did you find us?"* she asked.

"We heard from someone that there was a *habesha* family that had just arrived, and that they were pent up in a motel and knew no one. We remember our first days in America, so we came."

They showed my mother how to make *injera* and *sebhi* using American utensils, and they left us with enough food for a few days.

Seventeen years later, they still hold a special place in our hearts.

On some days, neither our sponsors nor our angels came. We still feared our new country, so we would stay inside and entertain ourselves by telling stories. Other times, we kids would play catch with little pebbles.

It never took long before a stone went somewhere it shouldn't have, like my father's ear.

GO AHEAD, YOU SONS OF WOMAN! BREAK SOMETHING AND GET US THROWN INTO THE HOUSE OF IMPRISONMENT.

SIRAHKHA KEREKHA IYE: I WILL SHOW YOU YOUR WORK.

As we searched for safer things, we discovered the great mouthpiece of America, the television.

My siblings and I had seen a fuzzy black-and-white television once in the big Sudanese city of Gedariff. We had heard about it from our friends, and we squirmed through the crowd of Sudanese natives and *habesha* refugees to reach the rich man's small, dirt-floor room. Once there, we bunched in among 30 spellbound viewers and watched tiny dots struggle to form the outlines of boxers on the screen.

Now, as we turned on the TV in our motel room, we noticed immediately that American dots were much stronger than the ones in Sudan. They did not struggle to form the images on the screen. In fact, sometimes you couldn't see the dots at all, only perfect color images.

Although we saw what the images did, we could not understand what they said. The only one who could was my father, who was considered an educated man among our people and could half-speak an Ethiopian/British dialect of English.

He was appalled by what the television told him.

GOD SHOW MERCY ON US! DID YOU HEAR THAT? THE BOYFRIEND KILLED HIS GIRLFRIEND AND HER PARENTS, TOO. HE STABBED THEM MORE THAN FIFTY TIMES. WHAT KIND OF COUNTRY HAVE WE COME TO?

My mother turned her face toward the heavens and lifted her quivering hands, as if to draw in God's angels around her. We kept watching as the television displayed more footage of the girlfriend and her family.

THEY WARNED US OF THIS WICKEDNESS CALLED BOYFRIEND AND GIRLFRIEND BACK IN ADI. DOING WHAT YOU WANT, LIVING OUTSIDE

THE RULE, AND THE NEXT THING YOU KNOW, YOU HAVE A STRANGE SICKNESS OR THEY KILL YOUR FAMILY.

We changed the channel. The dots formed a white child, getting ready to go to school. His mother hunched over and scanned his face for dirt, wiping white filaments from under his eyebrows and dirt from off his face. The lesson was not lost on my mother.

Do you see this? Tewolde, Selamawi, Mehret. Take note. If you do not wash your face and comb your hair, if you have even one speck on your face, they will chase you away from the school.

We would have come to the States one year earlier, in 1982. We had already passed the infamous immigration tests, sold our six goats, and begun to say goodbye to our fellow villagers. But in the final days, right before we were to leave our village forever, my half-sister Mulu came from another region of Sudan, surprising us.

Although we were scheduled to depart in a matter of days, my father and mother refused to leave without her. They begged the immigration officials. *YOU HAVE CHILDREN, DON'T YOU? WOULD YOU GO TO*

*AMERICA AND LEAVE YOUR DAUGHTER ALONE IN
THIS REFUGEE CAMP?*

"Look," they told us, "World Relief agreed to work with
a family of five, not a family of six. They agreed to bring
you now, not later, and it's impossible for her to come with
you now. She has no paperwork."

World Relief was a U.S.-based Christian organization
that sought refugees from all over the world and helped
them to resettle in the United States.

Millions of my people had become refugees during the
30-year bloodbath between Ethiopia and Eritrea. Most had
fled to Sudan. Seeing their plight, World Relief had
mediated an agreement between the U.S. and Sudan to
resettle some of the refugees.

As part of the resettling process, World Relief would
have to identify American sponsors who would find the
refugees housing, furniture, jobs, medical treatment, and
schools—everything that they would need to get on their
feet.

But before a family could qualify for resettlement, it had
to pass the infamous tests. No one knew which answers
were right and which were wrong.

"Why do you want to go to America? What will you do
when you get there? Do you want to come back to your
country some day? Do you plan to work in America?"

Many clever interviewees had failed despite giving the same answers as those who had passed. Others had passed after giving the same answers as those who had failed.

My father made one thing clear as we headed into our interview: He would speak for all of us. *DON'T ANY OF YOU SAY A WORD OR I WILL MAKE YOU LOST. LET ME DO ALL THE TALKING.*

Apparently, he told the officials what they wanted to hear, and they told us what we wanted to hear: "You are going to America! To a city called Chicago."

The officials insisted that we had to leave Mulu behind because she had not applied with the rest of us. But my parents refused to leave her. Returning day after day, sometimes three times a day, my father wore down the officials until they finally caved in. She could come if we waited one year.

We waited, the year passed, and six of us started on our way: my father, Haileab, in his late forties; my mother, Tsege, in her mid-twenties; my half-sister, Mulu, in her late teens; my older brother, Tewolde, nine; my younger sister, Mehret, five; and I, Selamawi, almost seven years old.

After World Relief met us at the airport, they paid for us to stay in a motel in Chicago. Meanwhile, they searched for a church that would sponsor us.

They could not find a sponsor in the city of Chicago, so after two weeks they moved us to another motel in the suburbs, on Route 38. A World Relief caseworker named Beth Raney had agreed to find us a sponsoring church in the area.

The first time we saw Beth, we wondered how such a small woman could exude so much energy.

The first time Beth saw us, she saw trouble. My father lay shivering under a blanket, his head aflame in fever, and Beth, a nurse, realized instantly that he had malaria.

We did not have access to medical care, so she went to a physician friend to obtain the medication that my father needed.

She also met with the pastors of area churches and asked if their congregation would sponsor a refugee family of six.

While she searched for a sponsor, she visited several times a week, talking with my father in his broken English, trying to communicate with my mother through words, but succeeding more through hugs and smiles.

"I still remember looking at Haileab's and Tsege's eyes and seeing the deepest pain," Beth recalls. "The pain of people who have been torn away from their loved ones, from their culture, from their place in society, from everything that has ever given their life coherence and dignity. I tried to help them, talking often with Haileab, trying to get him to talk about his life in his homeland.

"I tried to talk with Tsege, but it was hard because she knew so little English and because she would always retreat to the other room with the children when I came. Her culture had taught her that only men could speak with important visitors. She did not realize that I considered her to be just as important as Haileab and myself."

Beth found a sponsoring church, the Bethel Presbyterian Church. Like the rest of Wheaton, the church was almost all white, and from our standpoint, all *haftamat*, or crazy-rich. Bethel went to work immediately on finding us an affordable home—no small task in Wheaton.

We lived in the second motel for seven weeks. Then, one day, our sponsors at Bethel told us we had a home.

We had no idea what to expect. We had spent the previous three years living in a one-room adobe, and even then, we were grateful that we had the one room.

So when we saw our two-story house with its huge yard, we could not believe our eyes. *ARE THEY RIGHT? IS IT FOR REAL? THIS WHOLE STRETCH OF HOUSE AND YARD OURS? IT'S TOO MUCH.*

We could not afford the rent, even when my father had his job, so we rented out the entire upstairs. And then, a few months into our new home, our lives changed forever.

My parents went to the hospital. Our sponsors took us kids to their home. Two days later, my mother returned with a most precious gift. Conceived in Sudan but born in the States, he was a child of both the old and new worlds.

HIS NAME SHALL BE HNTSA-EYESUS, BUT HE WILL ALSO BE KNOWN AS TEMESGEN, OR THANK YOU. FOR WE ARE THANKFUL TO HAVE MADE IT HERE SAFELY, AND THANKFUL FOR OUR NEW LIFE IN THIS LAND.

Playground Warfare

From our very first days in America, my mother and father hammered into our minds the importance of excelling in school.

RIGHT NOW, WE ARE AMONG THE POOREST IN THE LAND. NEITHER YOUR MOTHER NOR I WILL FIND GOOD WORK BECAUSE WE LACK SCHOOLING. WE WILL HAVE TO WORK BACK-BREAKING JOBS, WE WILL NEVER FULLY UNDERSTAND OUR RIGHTS, AND OTHERS WILL TAKE ADVANTAGE OF US.

BUT IF YOU, OUR CHILDREN, WORK HARD AT SCHOOL AND FINISH THE UNIVERSITY, MAYBE SOMEDAY YOU CAN HELP YOURSELVES AND HELP YOUR FAMILY, TOO.

My parents may not have known much about this country, but they knew that the university cost more money than they had.

They had a solution, though. They told us that if we were among the best students in the land, we could earn scholarships and attend the university for free – in spite of our race and background.

YOU ARE POOR AND BLACK AND WE CANNOT BUY YOU THE RESOURCES THAT OTHER PARENTS CAN. BUT IF YOU HAVE ENOUGH DESIRE TO

27

OUTWORK ALL THE OTHER STUDENTS AND YOU NEVER GIVE UP, YOU WILL WIN THE RACE ONE DAY.

What's both beautiful and scary about young children is that they will believe most anything that their parents tell them. If our parents had told us that black refugees growing up on welfare in an affluent white community couldn't excel, we probably would have believed them.

But they told us that we could do anything if we worked hard and treated others with respect. And we believed them.

Sometimes, though, faith was not enough. No one taught us that lesson quite like our classmates at Longfellow Elementary School.

They had never seen anything like us, with our thick, perfectly combed afros, our perfectly mismatched clothing, and our spanking-new XJ-900's, bought from Payless Shoe Source for under $7 a pair.

My brother Tewolde and I patrolled the same playground for the hour-long lunch recess. Kindergarten met for just a half-day, so my sister Mehret went home before recess.

Most of our classmates treated us nicely, others ignored us, and the rest—well, we could only wish that they would ignore us. We may not have understood their words, but we always understood the meaning behind their laughter.

"African Boodie Scratcher! Scratch that Boodie!"

"Black Donkey! You're so ugly!"

"Why don't you go back to Africa where you came from?"

We were just two, and they were often many. But they had grown up in a wealthy American suburb, and we had grown up in a Sudanese refugee camp. We were accustomed to fighting almost daily, using sticks, stones, wood chips, and whatever else we could get our hands on.

So it was usually no contest, especially when the two of us double-teamed them, as we had done so many times in Sudan.

Sometimes, though, our classmates found us alone. One time, a brown-haired, overweight third grader named Sam cornered me along the north fence of the playground.

All about the school, kids played soccer, kickball, and four-square. We had but one supervisor to monitor the hundreds.

I don't remember what I had done to infuriate Sam; maybe it was something that Tewolde had done, and I was going to pay for it. Whatever the answer, Sam wanted to teach me a lesson.

He bellowed at me, getting louder with every word, until his face blossomed red. He bumped me against the fence and gripped the railing with his thick, chunky hands, sandwiching me in between.

I pushed against him desperately and tried to wiggle out, but he kept squeezing harder and harder, until the metal fence began to tear into my back, leaving me unable to breathe.

I searched for the supervisor but could not spot her. Nor could I see my brother. Fearing that Sam meant to squeeze all the life out of me, I started to cry for help. He squeezed even harder.

I think one of my brother's friends must have told him that Sam was suffocating me, because through the tears, I saw Tewolde exploding toward us. He came charging from the other side of the playground with all the fury of an angry bull.

Tewolde was half of Sam's size but he showed no hesitation. Without slowing, Tewolde leaped up, cocked his hand back and smashed it against the side of Sam's thick head.

Sam slumped to the asphalt and started to cry. But my brother had only started. He clenched his teeth and pounced on Sam's outstretched body, battering his face with punch after punch until Sam started to bleed.

I saw the supervisor coming toward our side of the playground, so I grabbed Tewolde and pulled him off. *Come on! Nahanigh, Tewolde! We have to go! Come on, before the supervisor sees us!*

Many battles later, my brother graduated to the fourth- and fifth-grade playground and left me to fend for myself. My younger sister Mehret was still on my playground, but she was small, too small to fight.

Mehret was so small that one day the strong wind picked her up and slammed her into the fence. My father berated the school administrators for not doing more to help her. But what could they do? She was small, and the wind was strong.

With time, I started to make friends through the soccer games at recess. Although my parents could not afford to put me on a team, Sudan had taught me well, with its days spent playing *kiesoh igre,* or *ball of foot.*

My brother met a good-natured white kid named Brian Willmer who lived right up the street from us. Brian became my brother's best friend and a great friend to everyone in our family. He came over to our house often, always telling us that we should send pictures of Hntsa to baby modeling agencies because Hntsa was so cute.

We made other friends, too, and started to fit in better. But the old enemies did not disappear. They had new ammunition, too. Every day, the TV news would broadcast explicit footage of famine-stricken Ethiopians.

"Hey, Salami! You look so skinny. Let me know if you need more food. You want another sandwich? How about some extra milk? I don't want you to starve."

It was even worse for my sister Mulu, who had to brave high school by herself. Her classmates drew skeletons on her locker and even serenaded her with the popular famine fundraising song, "We Are the World." She fought back until Wheaton North suspended her.

Tewolde and I even had confrontations with the only other Africans at our school: big, puffy-cheeked Frank and small, silent Mbago, a pair of brothers from Nigeria.

Both were in second grade with me, even though Frank was three years older than the rest of our class. How could that be?

None of us knew for sure, but we knew that he wasn't too bright. He used to pay other second graders to do simple math problems for him—five minus three, eight minus four, six plus seven—all for two cents a problem.

Even though we were from different countries, we still should have been brothers, defending and helping each other. But like our brothers in Africa, we were making war when we should have been making peace.

I tried to avoid them by playing on the opposite side of the playground.

But Mbago always provoked me. I think that he disliked me because I was poor and looked it, and he was ashamed to be African with me. When Frank was there, I had no choice but to let Mbago call me any names that he wanted. But whenever I found Mbago alone, and Mbago said anything mean to me, I always pounced on him and made him cry.

Invariably, he would return with Frank. They would corner me far away from the supervisor, when I least expected it, and beat on me until I had escaped or they had had enough.

They lived just down the street from us, less than one block away, so one day my bro and I hid in some bushes and waited for them with long, lean sticks in our hands. We would show them, Sudanese-style.

We sprang on them. *Slash. Scream. Slash.* They ran desperately.

But we were faster and cut them off. And Tewolde let out his anger. *Don't you ever touch my little brother again or you'll get it even worse!*

We strutted back home, victorious, even laughing as we recounted the incident.

33

But then we thought of whom they might tell, and our laughter stopped in a hurry. We retreated into our house, afraid of what we had done.

When we heard the frenzied knocking on our door, we knew that our time was up.

Their parents stood outside, guarding bruised and teary-eyed children. My parents yelled out in anger for us to appear. *DID YOU DO THIS? DON'T YOU DARE LIE OR I WILL MAKE YOU LOST RIGHT THIS MOMENT!*

Lifting us by our ears, my parents screamed at us and threatened us until the Nigerian parents had been appeased. Then the parents began talking about Africa, immigration, and all of the things they had in common.

"Would you like some *injera*? How about something to drink? That's all you are going to eat? How about some tea? Please. Visit us anytime you want. Of course not! Do not call first. You know that our people do not believe in appointments; come over whenever you want!"

It was the start of a beautiful friendship.

As Tewolde and I got older, the violence at school continued. So we kept defending ourselves—until the school administrators had no choice:

"This notice is to inform you that your children are fighting almost every day. Especially Tewolde. If they continue to fight with their classmates, we will have to consider expelling them from Longfellow Elementary School." Signed, Ms. Cobb, the principal.

My father sat, saying nothing, as he was known to do in moments of great crisis. Then he proclaimed his iron verdict.

YIIIIEEEEEE. ALL THIS COMING FROM ADI FOR THE SAKE OF SCHOOL AND EDUCATION, ALL FOR NOTHING.

LISTEN TO ME, MY CHILDREN. I AM YOUR FATHER, RIGHT? THEN LISTEN. I KNOW THAT IN SUDAN, YOU HAD TO FIGHT OR THEY WOULD KEEP BEATING YOU DAY AFTER DAY. WE ARE NOT IN SUDAN ANYMORE.

HERE IN AMERICA, THEY TAKE A SIMPLE THING LIKE A BRUISE AND KICK YOU OUT OF SCHOOL AND EVEN THROW YOU INTO THE HOUSE OF IMPRISONMENT. SO FROM NOW ON, LET THEM HIT YOU. COME HOME BEATEN AND BRUISED. DO NOT EVER FIGHT BACK.

My brother and I were dumbfounded. At best, we had expected screaming; at worst, the leather belt. But we had never imagined a betrayal of this magnitude. Our father, better than anyone, knew the importance of standing up for yourself.

We begged. We pleaded. We reasoned. What if they knock our teeth out? What if they make us bleed? What if they break our bones? If we let one kid beat us up, they're all going to beat us up.

DO YOU THINK THAT I WISH HARM ON MY CHILDREN? WE HAVE NO CHOICE. WE ARE POOR.

IF YOU GET EXPELLED, WHO WILL DRIVE YOU TO YOUR NEW SCHOOL? IF YOU GET EXPELLED, WHO WILL GIVE YOU A SCHOLARSHIP? DO YOU THINK THAT THEY GIVE SCHOLARSHIPS TO STUDENTS WHO GET EXPELLED FROM SCHOOL?

REMEMBER THAT THIS COUNTRY RUNS ON COMPUTERS. ONCE YOU COMMIT THE SMALLEST CRIME, YOUR NAME WILL BE STAINED FOREVER.

SO I'M TELLING YOU: IF THEY COME AFTER YOU, RUN. IF I EVER HEAR THAT YOU HAVE BEEN IN A FIGHT, FEAR FOR YOUR BEINGS. I WILL MAKE YOU LOST.

We feared my father more than anything in the world, so as painful as it was to stop fighting, we stopped fighting.

We learned to take taunting and small beatings. There were a few isolated incidents, though, where we had no choice but to defend ourselves.

There was the time that I was in fourth grade and my brother had graduated to middle school. Our neighbors, the Panther family, gave my sister Mehret rides because they had one extra seat in their station wagon. That left me to make the one-mile walk home by myself.

One day, two of my classmates, a light-skinned black kid named Dennis and a skinny white kid named Marc, jumped me on the way home. They would have given me a black eye and maybe more, worse than anything that awaited me at home. So I tightened my face into an angry scowl.

Feigning toward Dennis, I kicked Marc, hard as I could, XJ-900 right in his groin. Marc hunched over and whimpered to the ground. Dennis tried to run, but I caught him. I made sure that there would be no next time.

Dennis and Marc were easy pickings, but a year later, my brother met a more serious challenge: Jake Evans. Tough, mean, unstable, Jake was the deadliest kid at Franklin Middle School.

He was the school's head burnout, one of those heavy-metal white kids who did drugs and didn't care about anything. He struck fear in the entire student body. And he hated my brother.

Jake started telling everyone in the school that my brother's days were numbered. I rarely saw my brother tremble, but he trembled when he heard Jake's threat. He was right to tremble. Jake had about 80 pounds and a foot on him.

But what terrified us wasn't Jake's size. It was his illegal-length switchblade. We knew Jake had it because we had seen him practice with it, setting up targets in the grass near Triangle Park, hitting dead center almost every time.

Even if my brother could have taken Jake, Jake had seven or eight burnout lackeys who followed him around. My bro couldn't possibly survive all of them and their knives.

Eventually, the day came, as in one of those movies where the whole school knows that a student is going to get whooped.

My brother fidgeted all day long, trying to figure out an escape route. But there was no escape route. Too many people were watching him, talking about the fight. By the end of the day, everyone followed him home, including Jake.

Jake and his friends surrounded Tewolde about a block away from the school. My brother had a few friends around, but not nearly enough to save him. So he made a desperate prayer: *Dear God, please save me. Dear God, please save me. Dear God, just don't let them use their knives.*

I guess that God must have heard my brother because He sent some friends down to help him. A van pulled up, carrying four tall black guys. They looked like high-school students, maybe older. They strutted toward us with dangerous confidence.

"What's going on here? Does someone have a problem with our brother?"

No answer. Confronted with someone larger than himself, the school bully became the school coward.

"Why are you so quiet now, you little punk? Yeah, you. Don't look around like I'm talking to somebody else. I'm talking to you. If you touch this kid today or any other day, you're dead meat. You got that? Good. Now get the heck outta here."

Jake and his friends slunk away, never to be heard from again. They understood violence and they understood threats.

Those four rescuers? They were the older brothers of Tewolde's friend, Kawaun. Kawaun had told his brothers that all the white burnouts were getting together to gang up on his black friend, and his brothers had come down to help the black kid out.

At night, when we were still in elementary school, my brother told me the most hilarious stories. They usually starred these five Chinese brothers who had moved to the

United States. Each brother had his head shaved in the front and long hair in the back, sometimes braided. All five brothers lived together.

Tewolde spun his stories from the top bunk and I heard them from the bottom. They always featured the same plot: The five Chinese brothers craved peace and usually tried to mind their own business. But some ill-willed Americans would always mistreat them.

Like all Chinese people, the Chinese brothers had mastered kung fu, karate, and every other martial art. My brother and I knew this about Chinese people because of a TV show called "Samurai Sunday" that came on right after church. All the Chinese people in that show could really fight.

Tewolde's Chinese brothers would be doing something innocent, such as watering their garden, and then, out of nowhere, their neighbors would insult them or hurl a rock through their window. Having no choice, the Chinese brothers would use their kung fu to beat up the Americans.

Eventually, it got so bad that the brothers had to whoop the whole town; every last citizen, five citizens at a time. It was a lot of work, but the brothers had no choice.

Sometimes I wonder why my brother and I loved the Chinese brother stories. I used to think it was because they were funny.

Lately, though, I have come to believe that the brothers were more than stories. They were our kid way of dealing with our unfriendly world.

Even if we couldn't beat up all of the cruel kids at school, the five Chinese brothers could. They could whoop the kids, they could whoop their parents, they could whoop the entire town.

The Camp

Sometimes when we lay in bed, Tewolde and I shared other stories. Stories of our childhood in the refugee camp. Of old friends there and old enemies. Of our life and our family's life.

Hard though that life had been, we sometimes missed it.

Many of our people had gathered in Umsagata, a dusty village of straw-and-mud adobes.

Most of us survived on goat milk, chicken eggs, U.N. rations, and whatever we could grow in our small gardens. A Swedish ministry provided health care, and about a mile away sat a schoolhouse.

We took some brutal beatings at the schoolhouse. But these didn't come at the hands of bullies. Our kindergarten teachers could dish out pain, too.

I still remember the jealous, one-armed math teacher, who beat me senseless with his good arm because I had more right answers than his son.

He and the other teachers could punish us for almost any reason. Whereas parents in the States often defend their kids against the teacher, parents in Sudan took the teacher's side.

With few checks on their power, the Sudanese teachers didn't hesitate to pound us.

Get up! Hold your hands together! Now interlock your fingers so the knuckles are exposed.

Pulling the ruler back overhead, the teacher would unwind and slam torture into our naked knuckles, the ruler's metal edge knifing deep into our flesh. *Quiet! Hold your mouth or you will get more.*

Violence wasn't restricted to the classroom, either. Some of the other kids tried to push us around, so Tewolde and I quickly mastered Sudanese-style fighting, where the only object was survival. You used whatever was within reach because you knew that your rival would. Sticks. Stones. Sand. You had to use it and you had to win. I fought almost daily and still wear the scars. But I decorated a few bodies, too.

During some of the fights, we got help from our dog. I forget his name but I think it started with an 'H.'

H really made a difference one time, when Ahferom the village bully came looking for Tewolde and me. We tried to run. But it was too late—Ahferom grabbed my shirt and Tewolde had to stay to help me.

Before Ahferom could get started, though, we heard deep-throated snarling, the rapid tearing of fabric, a blood-curdling human scream.

Ahferom hobbled off, crying all the way home. H had rescued us by biting through Ahferom's pants, right into the dark flesh of his buttock.

We usually didn't believe in pets. How could we feed pets when all around us, our countrymen struggled to feed themselves?

No, all livestock—from the goat all the way down to the chicken—had to produce for their living. That's why my father strung our first dog on the clothesline in our backyard. My father had caught him killing the chickens one night when he was supposed to be watching them.

After H saved us from Ahferom, though, he assumed near-pet status. We pampered him. We played games with him. We took him with us when we went hunting with our slingshots.

We didn't use store-made, rubber-and-elastic slingshots, either. No, we used the same kind of slingshot that David used to drop Goliath. Just a narrow strip of cloth, folded in half the long way, with a stone placed inside the fold. Spin the cloth as fast as you can until it blurs up, and at maximum centripetal force, release the stone with a quick jerk of your wrist.

To hit a stationary object, especially one as small as a bird, required skill. To hit a moving one required tremendous skill and a good dose of luck. My brother had both.

One day he saw a bird flying and instantly let loose. Bird met ground. And then the pan. My mother cooked it up for us, and Tewolde, Mehret and I gathered around to devour it. But Ahferom came and asked to taste just a little bit.

It is unheard of in our culture to refuse people food, so we invited him to join us. He grabbed the whole bird and ran. HE ATE OUR BIRD!

At the time, we were furious. But in retrospect, I feel no anger. How can I feel ill will toward Ahferom when I know that soon after, he joined one of the Ethiopian liberation movements? And that later, he joined the long list of senseless casualties, able to survive our crazed dog but not his own countrymen?

Umsagata had no paved roads, so it didn't attract many cars. We walked or ran everywhere we went.

One time, though, a giant tractor pulled up. It was unlike anything that we had ever seen. Its wheels were the size of small adobes!

After awhile, the owner got out and entered a home. We ran over to inspect the tires, wondering if what we had heard was true: that if you took a sharp stone and applied pressure to the tire's little air nozzle, you could empty out all of the air.

We grabbed little stones and pushed eagerly. Sure enough, the air shot out of the tire like lava from a volcano.

The owner shot outside, shaking his fists in fury. We bolted. For we knew that no tire pumps could be found anywhere nearby. And who wants to be stuck in the middle of Sudan with a flat, giant tractor?

No doubt, Tewolde and I were mischievous. But we weren't nearly as dangerous as our friend Kiros. He was only six but could climb any tree, no matter how tall. Fifty feet. Sixty feet. One hundred feet! No problem. And he loved stones. So he would climb trees with stones in his pocket and pick off whomever passed by.

All of us made room for him at our tables, knowing that with one stone, he could take our eyes out. Even the old woman who peddled peanuts next to the clinic shared her wares with him.

After two years, Kiros left Umsagata for a faraway paradise. I think his dad called it AmeriKHA.

Many refugees died from sickness, and at one point, a deadly disease called *kahlazar* invaded my body. Neither food nor rest nor medicine seemed to help. I remember approaching death and being carried around at night, through the dusty roads and thatched adobes of our *habesha* village, through the solemn silence of the neighboring Muslim village.

With time, though, my body recovered.

On days such as my recovery day, or on religious feasts, we threw parties with all of our camp's *habesha* villagers. We danced our circle dance, moving our shoulders emphatically to the steady beat. We used no synthesizers or drum sets— just a goat-hide drum and a goat-hide guitar.

To the best dancers went more than admiration. Spectators moistened bills and slapped them enthusiastically on the best dancers' heads.

My father knew how to dance with every muscle in his body—shoulders, arms, hands, back, knees, feet, legs. Even his face gyrated in perfect rhythm with the drum and the guitar.

Villagers always interrupted their business when he joined the dancers' circle. Conversations stopped. Cups lowered. Heads turned. Then the villagers jumped from their seats and plastered him with money, until bills decorated his head, his neck, and even his clothes.

He was hands-down the best dancer in our village—the best dancer of *habesha* music that I have ever seen. Even in the States, when my father had lost much of his eyesight and coordination, my *habesha* friends would always watch him in wonder. "If I could dance like that," they would say, "I wouldn't need anything else. Women would just drop at my feet."

When the dancing finished, we would return to our one-room adobe, where my entire family slept. My mother, who knew how to scare young children into proper behavior, always told me that if I let the covers down, snakes could slither into my mouth and enter the rest of my body. She said that it had happened to a little boy in our neighboring village.

I believed her and instantly started pulling the covers over my head. I still do it today.

Unfortunately, my family had much more to fear than imaginary snakes. Sudanese rebel groups waged their own war against the Sudanese government, and we wondered about our village's safety. We also didn't know how long we could dodge the diseases that had conquered so many of our countrymen.

One thing was certain: We could not seek safety in our homeland. The Eritrean liberation groups continued their quest for independence and were joined by other Ethiopian liberation forces. If we returned home, my parents believed, we would be wiped out by the Dergue army of Ethiopian dictator Mengistu Haile Mariam.

So it was that my father started talking about this land called AmeriKHA. He told us that money grew on trees in AmeriKHA. Everyone was rich. Everyone had a home. Everyone had food. And everyone had peace.

Everyone lived to be 100 years old. And had access to free education. And no wars—no wars! Yes, everyone had cars, and no one had to work more than a few hours.

What a country! What a paradise!

But such a faraway paradise included no relatives, no friends, and no one who spoke our language. Some villagers encouraged my father to go; others begged him to stay.

"Have you lost your mind, Haileab? Don't you care about your children? Don't you care about yourself?"

"Don't believe all the stories. You will be lost if you go there. You and your children will be lost. You'll end up washing their mules and other livestock."

"Go, Haileab. Don't listen to them. Go, and take your family with you. Even if you remain poor, your children will become educated, and at the very least, you will have peace."

Would you go to paradise if it meant knowing no one? Would you give up everything you had ever known?

My parents made their decision, and the truck rumbled toward us. It was a lorry, one of those mammoth vehicles that looks like an African elephant. Its gaping back entrance beckoned us, giving us advice. Oh, that we could have heard it!

Come on in. Come, if you dare.

Make your choice carefully, for once you enter, you cannot return.

Turn and look at your friends, and know that they are your true family. For friends and even enemies become family when you live in exile.

Look at them and know that you will never see them again. Wave goodbye to H. Go hug him.

Believe it or not, you will miss even the bullies and the cruel math teachers. For even the most horrifying memories are you; they are yours and no one else's. And they, along with the good memories, are your life.

You know America through stories. You know it to be paradise. But beware! Rumors are malignant tumors. Snakes lurk even in paradise. And the advice of mothers does not always ward off evil.

Look back, too. You have survived many dangers. Famines. Diseases. Wars. Despair. Homesickness and more. Who knows what your future will bring?

We entered the lorry slowly. Behind us, our village waved, both happy and terrified for us. And for themselves, too.   We waved goodbye, and the lorry rumbled off, a bloated country taxi, jam-packed with hopeful innocents.

We made our way through the Sudanese wilderness, up and down the hills, to Gedariff.

We spent several months in Gedariff.   Then a week in the capital city, Khartoum.

Then we entered the plane and took off from Khartoum.   The next stop was Athens.   Then AmeriKHA, and there, a new life.

God's Angels

We were just starting our life in AmeriKHA when our father told us about strangers. We should always treat them kindly, he said, because they could have been sent by God. He told us stories of how back home in *Adi*, God's angels would descend out of mountains and mingle among the people.

But people always mistreated the angels, my father said, because the angels never looked like angels. They were always disguised as beggars, homeless dangers, and misfits.

But no matter how abnormal or smelly the strangers, my father always maintained that they could be angels, given to us by God to test the deepest sentiments of our hearts.

When we were but infants in our new home, my father welcomed an angel into our house. This angel was particularly well-disguised. He emitted the most ungodly odor, half from his nasty clothes and half from his smudged and muddy body. He walked with a great weariness, as if he were about to collapse with each step, and his spirit had almost abandoned his eyes.

Maybe because my father had been an angel himself so often; maybe because he had often survived only because of those who could see through his disguise; maybe because he had felt the deep pain of homelessness—my father welcomed

52

the man into our home. We fed him and clothed him and gave him shelter.

This angel did not have much; in fact, it looked like he had absolutely nothing. But as he left, he gave us a gift.

He pulled a rainbow-colored address book out of his dirty shirt and handed it to us. We refused, but he insisted. And we accepted. For we knew that the exchange of gifts blesses the giver even more than the receiver. And even though we were not familiar with address books and had not used them before, we used his address book to store the addresses and phone numbers of our loved ones for the next several years. And we always thought of him: our angel.

Most angels don't look like angels. But a few do. A 20-year-old angel with a celestial face and long, streaming, brown hair floated into our lives right after the other angel departed. I don't remember when she first came to us, but I remember her visits.

We would be cooped up in the house, our parents too scared to let us play outside and too scared to take us around themselves. And then, she would come. I don't know why my parents trusted her. Maybe that's why she looked like an angel, so that they would trust her.

She would take us to play soccer at Wheaton College, where she went to school, then to the playground, and then she would pull out her acoustic guitar and sing to us. Sing with us, sing to us. Then she would teach us of the lamp that guides all paths. Tewolde and Mehret and I were just kids. Maybe that's why we saw her for what she was and still keep her in our hearts countless heartbeats later.

If you are out there, Charlene, and are reading this, I know your heart of gold weeps and smiles. Know that we have often thought of you and looked for you. When we look, we always look toward the heavens, for we know that is your true home. You are but a visitor here.

Days of Mischief

Each year we spent in Sudan, on a day that every kid looked forward to, our little village erupted into a sea of flames.

We built a huge bonfire in the middle of the village. We gathered thick sticks and dipped them into the fire, pulling them out only after they had blazed into torches. Then we raced together from adobe to adobe.

Muslims and Christians, Eritreans and Ethiopians, bullies and prey—on this night, all of us forgot our differences and united. We ran from adobe to adobe, waving our torches fearlessly, chanting out our ancestors' cry:

Hoyo Hoyo, Hoyo
Hoyo Hoyo, Hoyo
Akho Akhokay, Berhan Geday
Berhan Neibel, Hoyo,
Himaq Wisa, Hoyo,
Quincha Wisa, Hoyo,
Tekwon Ito, Hoyo,

"Oh, new year, let it be a good one, all the evil leave us, let peace join us, let harvest come."

Our parents waited for us at their adobes and chimed in enthusiastically when we approached, *Hoyo Hoyo, Hoyo! Hoyo Hoyo, Hoyo!*

They told us that in the old days, in the old country, before the rise of Mengistu and the Dergue and desolation, adults passed out presents to the children during *Hoyo Hoyo.* Money, candy, food, and even home-brewed liquor for the older kids.

But in our refugee camp, no one could afford to give presents to so many.

Presents or no, we still loved *Hoyo Hoyo.* On this one day, we embraced what we most feared on other days.

You can't hurt us today, oh, fire. We say IMBEE! NO YOU CAN'T! Go ahead. Burn us and our adobes. Take our chickens and goats, and even our gardens.

For today, we are not refugees, we don't live in adobes. No, we live back home among our people, and we celebrate our new year, and we dance with you like our forefathers before us.

When we came to America and heard of a strange holiday where children morphed into all manner of strange creatures, my siblings and I were puzzled. But eventually, we understood. This was their version of *Hoyo Hoyo.* Just like we did, they roamed from house to house and brought smiles to adults. Instead of *Hoyo Hoyo*, they chanted "Trick or Treat!" Instead of fire, they flouted vampires, witches, and all of Hell's creatures.

Our refugee village in Sudan could not afford presents, but this country gladly showered candy, fruit, even money on its petitioners.

And not just a little bit of candy, but almost unlimited free candy—beyond our wildest dreams! Declaring Halloween our favorite holiday, we convinced our parents that they should allow us to go trick-or-treating alone. By the second year, we had our strategy all figured out.

We raced through Wheaton's quiet streets, all the way home from school, arriving home before any of our classmates. After ransacking our parents' closet for two pillowcases, we started out on our way—usually with hastily designed costumes. One year, I took a grocery-sized paper bag, poked two holes in it and dubbed myself, "Paper Bag Man."

We had two rounds. During the treasure round we did not knock on any doors. We ran from house to house, searching eagerly for baskets labeled, "Please take one." Without pausing, we snatched the baskets and dumped all of their contents into our bags.

We wondered sometimes, did adults really expect unsupervised kids to take only one piece of candy? What self-respecting kid would do such a thing?

We started round two right as most kids started their regular trick-or-treating. We joined them in running from house to house, crying out with our *habesha* accents: TREEHK OHR TREET! We usually received our candy graciously and made sure to say TANKOOH.

But we weren't always nice. Each year, we singled out several round-two victims for some special fun.

One year we saw two white boys sitting on their front steps. They sat, talking softly, laughing, their bright, blond hair stirring in the early evening wind. Tewolde and I laughed as we sized them up, taking in their neatly pressed clothing and their bright, honest faces.

The straw basket they guarded dwarfed the youngest boy. But what was in it? What treasures did that basket hide? Lollipops? Tootsie Rolls? Candy bars? We hoped that it wasn't fruit so we wouldn't have to throw it back at their house later.

We approached the house. When we saw the orange rectangles brimming over the basket's top, we felt our stomachs growl. It was our favorite: Reese's Peanut Butter Cups. There had to be one hundred Reese's in that treasure box. Two hundred. Who knows, it might have even been five hundred! Certainly enough for several months!

We had seen the two boys once before with their dark metallic bikes. Their bikes glimmered with an even brighter shine than new bikes; we knew that they must have spent hours every day, cleaning them.

Any kid who cleaned his bike every day would be easy picking, so we approached quietly, knowing that this would be fun.

I slid around to the back of the house, keeping low, making sure that they didn't see me.

Tewolde approached the house. He stopped out on the sidewalk and motioned the kids over excitedly. "Hey, come look at this."

The older kid hesitated a little bit. I couldn't wait for him to go. All I needed were a few seconds.

He went.

And I shot out from my hiding place, straight for the Reese's. The younger one screamed, but it was too late. I was already dumping the basket into my pillowcase.

I couldn't get it all because the older kid heard the scream and started to run back. Above all, I feared that their parents might come out.

But we still got about half of that candy, and I split it with Tewolde once we were several blocks away.

I couldn't have known it then, but I would run into that older kid again.

Several Halloweens after we pirated the Reese's, our friend Kiros from the Sudanese village joined us in Wheaton. He would make Tewolde and me look like Mother Teresa.

Kiros lived with us for a few weeks and then relocated next to our Cambodian and Vietnamese refugee brothers down on Route 38, in the yellow-and-red-brick apartments that house most of Wheaton's refugees.

We wondered, "Is he still crazy? Does he still climb huge trees and launch missiles down onto unprotected heads?"

Soon after he arrived, Kiros and I sat in the basement of my family's home, playing *Gifa*, a card game we had learned in Sudan. Playing led to cheating, cheating to yelling, yelling to card-throwing, and I arose, ready to defend myself. Kiros was no bigger than me.

But he leaped up. And grabbed a plastic baseball bat. Swinging it wildly and swearing injury, he lunged at my head. I bolted for the stairs. He was still crazy.

After Kiros moved down to Route 38, we did not see him as often. Sometimes he vanished for weeks, even months.

But each October 31, no matter how long it had been, his thick afro always greeted us at our door after school. How he beat us home, we never quite figured out, since our schools let out at the same time and he had much farther to run. I guess he feared that we would start without him or forget about him.

The three of us started on our way. Was it us or my parents who refused to let Mehret come along? Probably my parents, since they are *habesha*, and *habeshas* never let their daughters do anything.

Rounds one and two merged into one with Kiros along. Tewolde egged us on:

See that basket full of Snickers and Milky Ways inside the porch? That porch door looks open to me. I bet you it is—who locks their porches in Wheaton? I dare you to sneak inside and get that basket, man. Look at all those candy bars. I dare you. Do it if you're a man.

Watch out, Selamawi! Kiros is in! He's pouring the candy into his pillowcase. Run, dude, run! She's coming! He's got the basket and the fat white woman chases him. Goo-ye! Run before her husband comes! Run before the police find us! Run or our lives will be lost! Change blocks! Jump the fence!

Are you crazy, Kiros! I was just kidding! All right. At least share some of that candy for all of the running we had to do because of you.

We did many deeds that were downright dishonest, but we only felt guilty about one. And we didn't even mean to do that one.

We had approached a house and rung the doorbell, and when that didn't work, we started to knock on the door. Was anyone there? It was one of those long, narrow, single-level homes near the railroad tracks, and most of the lights were off.

Tewolde and I started to leave. *Wait,* Kiros said. *I see her coming. She's coming very slowly.*

The old woman hobbled to the door, peering outside before opening it. She held an aluminum tray of candy bars.

We bowed respectfully to her and put on our best smiles. In our culture, we never harm the elderly. We revere them. We rise and give them our seats if they enter a room. We refer to them in the plural, never the singular, for they have the wisdom and deserve the respect of many.

I went first and took one, just like she said. No Reese's, but my second-favorite, Snickers. Tewolde went next. He reached out his hand to take another Snickers.

We never quite figured out what happened next. Maybe Kiros pushed Tewolde, maybe Tewolde slipped, maybe the old woman slipped. Whatever the cause, Tewolde knocked the tray over and the candy bars scattered, some to Tewolde's bag, some to the grass, some to the startled woman's feet.

We bent down to gather the candy for her. *You clumsy chump, Tewolde. What did you do?*

We were trying to help her, but the old woman, convinced that we intended to rob her, raised the aluminum tray high overhead, like Moses about to shatter the Ten Commandments.

Ranting and raving and crying all at once, the old woman smashed the metal tray on Kiros' fro with frightening force.

Kiros slumped to the sidewalk, too dizzy to move. *Get up, Kiros. Get up!* We tried to drag him up and flee all at once.

The old lady hobbled after us but couldn't catch us. How could she when she could barely walk?

We had felt guiltless in taking from those richer than us in Wheaton—maybe because taking was so much fun, or maybe because we considered ourselves modern-day Robin Hoods, taking from the rich and giving to the poor (ourselves).

But even we had rules. Rules forged by the limping refugee woman, by our own flight, by our handicapped father, by our mother's homesickness, by "African Boodie Scratcher," by the many harsh things we had known.

Our rules demanded that we would never add hurt to the hurting.

The old woman could not catch us, but she threw her words to track us down. We heard them and we trembled. For we had always been taught, and we earnestly believed, that the heartfelt curses of the elderly and the weak are heard by Him above, and that they always come true—if not in this world, then in the next.

As much as our run-in with the old woman shook us up, it didn't cure us of mischief. We still plundered many baskets and looted many trays.

It took something else, something completely unrelated to Halloween, to make us consider changing our ways. It took the parking meter.

It all started when basketball dethroned soccer as our favorite sport. Growing up in Michael Jordan's backyard, we started to play hoops religiously.

During the height of our basketball fever, all of Wheaton's teenage greats converged on one outdoor court: Triangle Park, just over the railroad tracks from where we lived.

We went to watch and play almost every day, each time crossing the railroad tracks illegally. We had heard that there was a $50 fine if you got caught, but we didn't care.

We refused to walk all the way around, more than 400 yards extra, just to use the crosswalk.

One day we crossed the tracks, walked through the trees, and came out on the other side, across the street from the rectangle that was misnamed Triangle Park. Close to 40 Vietnamese and Cambodian refugees, Wheaton College students, and Route 38 brothers milled about the court.

We knew that we would have to wait at least an hour to get a game. We stood on our side of the street, adding our figures to the long line of parking meters that guarded the tracks behind us.

Tewolde. Myself. A giant, light-skinned, Nigerian-American brother named Bo. And a dark-skinned brother with an impressive fro, even bigger than the ones that Americans had sported in the '70s. This was the kind of fro that Eritrean and Ethiopian *tegadalies*, or guerilla fighters, grew out in the wilderness.

Guerilla-afro brother leaned against the parking meter, and it moved. Not much, but just enough.

Glancing at the sand-speckled dirt next to the meter, and then at each other, each of us considered the same question: How many quarters did that double-headed parking meter hold?

"I bet it holds at least five dollars! Maybe even ten!"

"I bet it holds even more. The meter man probably comes to collect the money every two weeks, and with its two heads, the meter probably collects at least two dollars a day. There's gotta be at least 30 dollars in there."

Thirty divided by four equals seven dollars and fifty cents. Tewolde and I grinned at each other—this could double our annual budget!

Each time we went to Triangle Park, we shook our giant piggy bank just a little more. Each time, we heard our money jingle a little more freely.

One day Big Bo became impatient and bull-rushed the meter, knocking it flat on its feet.

Pedestrians and cars passed by, commuters coming home after a long day's work in the city. If they saw four brothers standing next to the fallen meter, they would suspect something. If they saw four brothers carrying it, they would call the police.

But we refused to leave our parking meter. We had worked too hard for it. And we wanted our $7.50.

We picked it up. One parking meter, four teenage guys—no problem, we figured.

But the city had weighed down the bottom of the meter with more than 100 pounds of cement, making it almost impossible to balance.

We didn't care. It could have been 300 pounds. Nothing was going to keep us from our money.

We dragged our prize to the secret tunnel next to the railroad tracks. Tewolde and I had discovered the tunnel long ago, when we had gone hunting with our Cambodian brother. Slinging homemade bows and arrows, we had patrolled the trees that border the tracks, looking for rabbits and squirrels. Once, we had hit a rabbit and it had led us to the tunnel.

The tunnel was a great underground hideaway. Usually, though, we avoided it because overgrown plants guarded the entrance and darkness reigned inside. Besides, the tunnel was only three feet high.

We crept in slowly, waiting for our eyes to adjust to the dark. We kept dragging the meter until we were sure that no one could see it from the outside.

Then we encountered our first major problem: We had no way to get the money out. The meter's money pouch had no screws near it. I guess the city had prepared for punks like us.

We returned the next morning with hammers, screwdrivers, and nails, vowing to find a way into the money pouch. We saw metal tent pegs lying next to the tracks; they would help us to pop open the meter head.

One hour elapsed, and still, we labored. To keep our spirits up, we shook the meter head and listened to the clang of our quarters. Laughing, we considered ourselves the boldest adventurers. Who could stop us?

At some point, I heard a noise. But I thought it was one of the others. As the static of the walkie talkie grew louder, though, I knew. I knew even before I saw the flashlight and the metal star and the white policeman's unbelieving face gazing in at us. I saw felony at age 11 flash before my eyes, and I saw it mirrored in my brother's eyes, too.

Even worse, we both thought of my father:

MY CHILDREN. THERE WAS A POOR WIDOW WHO LIVED IN THE COUNTRYSIDE. SHE HAD NEITHER LIVESTOCK NOR GARDEN AND LIVED EACH DAY WITHOUT KNOWING WHAT OR HOW SHE WOULD EAT THE NEXT DAY. SHE HAD ONLY ONE THING IN THE WORLD, HER YOUNG SON.

ONE DAY THE WIDOW'S SON, WHO HAD GROWN OLD ENOUGH TO PLAY OUTSIDE WITH HIS FRIENDS, BROUGHT HOME AN EGG. A TINY EGG—SMALL, LIKE THE DUST. THE WIDOW DID NOT ASK WHERE THE TINY EGG CAME FROM. SHE BOILED IT AND THEY ATE IT TOGETHER.

THE NEXT DAY THE SON BROUGHT A BIGGER EGG. SOON AFTER, TWO EGGS. THEN TEN EGGS. FINALLY, HE BROUGHT THE WHOLE CHICKEN. THE WIDOW STILL SAID NOTHING. SHE KEPT COOKING THE FOOD AND FEEDING HERSELF AND HER SON.

MANY CHICKENS, GOATS AND SHEEP LATER, THE SON FINALLY HIT THE JACKPOT: HE

*BROUGHT HOME A WHOLE COW. HIS MOTHER
SAID NOTHING AND THEY MILKED THE COW AND
DRANK THE MILK TOGETHER.*

*AS THEY SAT, FINISHING THE MILK, THE
MAGISTRATE CAME WITH THE POLICE AND
ARRESTED THE SON FOR STEALING THE COW.
DECLARING THAT THE SON WOULD HAVE TO DIE
FOR HIS CRIME, THE MAGISTRATE ORDERED THE
POLICE TO TAKE HIM TO THE HOUSE OF
IMPRISONMENT.*

*THE DISTRAUGHT WIDOW HUMBLED HERSELF
AND THREW HERSELF AT THE MAGISTRATE'S FEET
AND BEGGED FOR HER SON'S FREEDOM. "PLEASE,
SIR, I BEG YOU, HE IS MY ONLY SON AND ALL THAT
I HAVE. PLEASE SHOW MERCY ON HIM."*

*BUT BEFORE THE MAGISTRATE COULD SPEAK,
THE SON REPLIED TO HIS MOTHER: "NO,
MOTHER, IF YOU HAD REALLY CARED ABOUT ME,
YOU SHOULD HAVE STOPPED ME WHEN IT WAS
ONLY A TINY EGG. NOW IT'S TOO LATE."*

*IT STARTS SMALL, WITH A TINY EGG. BUT
BEFORE YOU KNOW IT, THE EGG BECOMES A
CHICKEN AND THE CHICKEN, A COW. THEN YOU
FIND YOURSELF IN THE HOUSE OF
IMPRISONMENT OR WORSE.*

SO I AM TELLING YOU NOW—DON'T SAY THAT YOUR FATHER DID NOT WARN YOU. IF I EVER CATCH YOU STEALING THE SMALLEST THING, IF I HEAR THAT YOU HAVE EVEN BEEN THINKING ABOUT STEALING ANYTHING, FEAR FOR YOUR LIVES.

I WILL MAKE YOU LOST.

Having attended church 50 Sundays out of the year and studied the Bible as a family each Saturday and Sunday night, having grown up with our culture's morals implanted in our conscience, and of course, having heard our father's "it starts with an egg" fable, we should have feared to steal anything, let alone government property.

But we had not learned our lesson, and we found ourselves staring at a policeman. Had he seen us looking for the tent pegs out on the tracks? Had a passerby heard the clanging and told him about the noise? Had he discovered the missing parking meter and decided to snoop around?

We didn't know. We just knew that it was time to run.

My brother and I had been chased by a huge dog one summer, chased for two blocks. We had run then.

We had exploded fireworks near a bully's foot one Fourth of July, and he had chased us for almost half a mile. We had run then.

But never in our lives had we run like we ran from that cop. Keeping our heads low, hoping that the policeman was too tall to fit in the tunnel, praying that another policeman did not wait on the other side, we blazed out of the tunnel, as if a time bomb ticked behind us.

We sprinted all the way home, flew into our rooms and changed our clothes. *Put on a hat! Pat down your hair! Try to look different! Hide in the basement!*

And pray that they don't come.

Libee Migbar

Even as we were vandalizing parking meters and terrorizing Halloween baskets, my brother and I were still what most Americans would call "good kids." We listened to our parents, we did our best in school, and God knows, we tried to respect our peers.

It hurt to see our parents struggle, and we wanted, more than anything, to be able to help them someday. So we worked hard at school, and after several years, we graduated from the ESL (English as a Second Language) program at Longfellow Elementary and entered regular classes full-time.

We were extremely fortunate to be in School District 200, where we were blessed with outstanding teachers. We recognized our luck and took advantage of it.

Over the next 10 years, my older brother and I missed fewer than 10 days of school combined.

During that time, we thought more and more about how we could help our family. That's when Tewolde really started to change.

Around age 13, he started to go through a special transformation, an emotional maturity that my people call *libee migbar*, or developing a heart.

His transformation would end up transforming us all.

Growing up, Tewolde and I often visited Wheaton Public Library. We made two particular visits that I'll never forget. The second came during the days of espionage, when we awoke at 4 a.m. to spy on the janitors.

The first one was different. It was January 1989, and we went with sandwiches, thick, poor-man's ham from Aldi's supermarket, slapped onto wheat bread and slathered with a thin film of mayonnaise. We approached the library's entrance and saw a dark-haired white brother shivering under the awning, where kids usually wait for their parents.

But he was no kid, and no one was coming for him. That's why he was sitting outside in the dead of winter.

We watched his reddish cheeks quiver; we couldn't tell if it was from the cold or from something else. We went to him and asked him if he was hungry, and he said, "I lost my job and never got another one, and I don't think I'll ever get one again. I'm done."

We couldn't tell if he was the address-book brother from long ago, but we knew in our hearts that it did not matter. Maybe every stranger was an address-book brother, sent to test the goodness in our hearts.

Whatever the answer, Tewolde's heart spoke: *We should give him our sandwiches.* I nodded my head and took the sandwiches out of my backpack. I offered them to him. *I hope you like Aldi ham, bro.*

I went inside then, but Tewolde stayed outside and braved the cold with our friend. A few minutes later, Tewolde and I left.

I forgot about the man for about a year, and I thought that Tewolde had, too. It turned out that he hadn't.

By the time my brother reached junior high, he had mastered the art of getting things for free. Even though we had an annual budget of less than $40, he still finagled Nintendos, Segas, and other rich-boy treasures from his friends and other sources.

We wanted to lift weights when we entered high school, so he set out looking for a bench and free weights. He found both at our free mall, the dumpsters of Wheaton College.

In the past, the dumpsters had given us everything from bikes, desks, and school supplies to couches and even TVs. Why go shopping? It was graduation time, and our free mall was stocked, as the middle- and upper-class students threw away most of their belongings.

A year later, a friend gave Tewolde another bench and more weights. We had more than we needed. So Tewolde asked me to help him: "I have a friend who needs these weights," he told me. "He's trying to get in shape but cannot afford workout equipment."

Hoping it wasn't far, I followed Tewolde. It was across the street—in the nightmare apartments I had visited in elementary school. I'd had a friend who lived in the building's cellar; it was the kind of cellar that made me think of turn-of-the-century factory workers. No lighting. No air. No life. How could such a place exist in Wheaton?

We dragged the bench, the bar, and the weights upstairs and knocked on the door. A malnourished man answered, and I tried to remember where I had seen him. But I couldn't place him.

When he saw my brother, his gaunt, joyless face burst wide with laughter.

"How did you get these?" he asked us, and my brother said we had an extra one. We stayed and talked for a few minutes, and he told us that he was trying to make it, trying to keep his job. But it was hard, so hard, to have confidence and hope.

As he talked, I came to realize who he was. And as we left, I asked my brother: *How did you know where to find the address-book brother from the library? Did you run into him again?*

But even as I asked, I knew the answer.

My brother had found him housing and a job, encouraged him, and even given him money when he could—even though my bro had so little himself. All of this, without telling anyone.

The second time we went to the library, in the days of espionage, arose from earlier days, when my brother and I had worked like indentured servants. We had been too young to work real jobs, and even if we had been old enough, we would have been deterred by my father's declarations.

COMPUTERS RUN THIS COUNTRY; YOU CANNOT DO EVEN ONE THING WITHOUT THE HOUSE OF AUTHORITY KNOWING ABOUT IT. SO IF YOU WANT TO WORK, YOU HAVE TO WORK CASH JOBS. IF YOU WORK CHECK JOBS, THEY WILL TRACE YOUR MONEY AND YOU WILL HAVE TO REPORT IT, AND THEN THEY WILL SIMPLY TAKE THAT MONEY OUT OF YOUR WELFARE CHECK AND YOU'LL BE BACK TO WHERE YOU STARTED.

To avoid the all-knowing computers, we worked cash jobs for a shifty brother who lived down the street from us on Route 38. He paid us $5 an hour cash to restore torn-up driveways.

He would pick us up in his junky, rust-colored pickup—the kind that Redd Foxx owned in the TV show "Sanford and Son"—and we would roam from home to home.

We always started by sweeping pebbles and dirt from the driveway and finished by sealing the cracks with tar. Laboring under the hot, summer sun, we fried.

You're getting darker, my mother would tell us. *This job is killing you, you should quit.* But $20 a day was too much to pass up, at least for a while.

Eventually, as luck would have it, my brother found our good friend, Jim Settacase. Jim ran his own cleaning service and he paid us with checks.

Despite the checks, working for Jim was worth it because he paid a whopping $7 an hour. More important, he toiled and smiled and laughed alongside us, until we almost looked forward to work.

I never saw my brother that summer because he worked nights, cleaning the Toyota dealership with Jim, and I spent all day flipping burgers and stirring fries.

Jim encouraged Tewolde and taught him to build from almost nothing. So at age 17, my brother ventured out and started his own cleaning business. *"Working for somebody* *else, we make $7 an hour, but working for ourselves, we can make up to $25!"*

Tewolde's business grew with the help of a high-school psychology teacher named Mr. Wimpleberg. He met with Tewolde after school and taught him how to market to different kinds of customers.

Tewolde passed on the lessons to me: *"You see, Selamawi, there are A-type customers, B, and then C. C brothers would never pay a dime to have someone clean for them; they are like us—they'll clean it themselves first. B brothers have enough money and can be convinced, and A, well, forget about it with A. That's where ALL the loot is."*

So my brother printed up his impressive black-and-white cards that said "ProClean: No One Cleans Better," and hey-hey, he was in business. Soon he had a chiropractor's office to clean—twice a week, $40 for two hours.

Soon after that he started cleaning windows—who could have imagined that you could get paid $75 to clean windows?—and then word spread about his business.

That's when he started to dream: *"Forget this fifty here and hundred there, let's make some real money. Selamawi, I think I can make $30,000. Maybe I shouldn't even go to college next year."*

So he looked for business opportunities and began staking out the three-floor Wheaton Public Library.

He awoke with the night cleaners, arriving right after them, and carefully documented their errors through the windows. Returning during the day, he snooped around some more and talked to the day janitor, whom he had known for years.

I told him he was crazy. *Look, bro, how many of them does it take to clean that place? I'm not gonna wake up at 4 a.m. to clean it with you—I gotta study and sleep and run cross country—and you can't do it by yourself.*

But he was determined. His new heart had been inspired by his faith in God, and he believed that God wanted him to try "impossible" things. He kept watching the janitors, hoping he could approach the library's management. One day, he might convince them that he would do a better job than the night cleaners.

But Tewolde never talked to the management, and he never graduated from high school. A drunk driver killed him midway through his senior year.

One close friend, our white grandma, brings him up every time we see her:

"You know, your brother was the most precious boy. I remember how at church, I would go up on the second floor after the service, and I would see all the high-school students. You know how high-school students are, they refuse to say 'Hi' to you if you are old, even if they know you and have known you for years, because it is not 'cool' to acknowledge old people.

"But your brother, no matter who that boy was with or how many people were in his way, he would always leave his group of friends and wade through the crowd to hug me and talk to me. His love knew absolutely no shame.

"He was a special boy, and if I had a son, I would have wanted him to be just like Tewolde."

He is often remembered among our *habesha* community, too, even though it's been almost eight years:

"Yes, he was a blessed one, *bruck neyroo, abey kirikeb—where can his like be found?*, that eldest son of Father Haileab."

"Listen, now, there was that one time when their mother had gone back to Adi, and I came over because some guests were coming and I had promised to help with the preparations.

"I came over and soon found myself overwhelmed with cooking the *sebhi* and *injera*, let alone doing everything else. And then that boy came.

80

"I did not ask him to help, but he came in like a whirlwind, washing the dishes, sweeping the floors, straightening out the living room, helping me prepare the food, asking me to sit down and rest. Before I knew it, he had done almost everything himself and wanted to know if he could do anything else."

Not long after his death, I went to his room and looked through some of his papers. A single picture stopped me. It showed a dark-haired South American boy, about five years old, with the warmest, brightest, most hopeful eyes, and the hint of a smile on his light-brown face.

I flipped the card over and read it: "Here is your child. Thank you for sponsoring him. With your twenty dollars a month, he goes to school, receives medical care, and eats healthy food."

I wondered how my brother had donated $240 a year to Compassion International, when he had so little money to spare. He was struggling to save money for college and was trying to help his family, too.

I thought of the Biblical tale, where a rich man donates a large sum to a synagogue and a poor woman donates her last two cents. As the story goes, her gift is worth infinitely more, for the rich man gave out of his surplus and she out of her scarcity.

As I reflected on what my bro had meant to the child, I thought of what he meant to all of us.

I thought of my mother, and her special relationship with him, and how when he was a child and misbehaved, she would grab the leather belt and try to whip him. But the harder she whipped him, the more Tewolde laughed, and the more he laughed, the harder she whipped him.

He would keep laughing, smiling at her with every blow, until she gave up and joined him in laughing.

I thought of our youngest brother, Hntsa. Tewolde knew that seven-year-old Hntsa loved quarters, so he would keep a lookout each night when he cleaned the Toyota dealership with Jim.

Tewolde always found several quarters—and if he didn't, he took some out of his own pocket—and left them in his shoes for Hntsa. As soon as Hntsa woke up, he would run to see how many quarters his older brother had left for him.

I thought of Mehret, the lone girl among us, who could always turn to Tewolde for an ally. I thought of my pops, and the high level of respect that Tewolde always showed him, even when doing so meant swallowing his own pride.

Then I thought of myself, and of what the word 'bro' means to me...

Mawi Asgedom

It means a measuring stick,
A higher standard,
A heart that sees angels,
A lifelong inspiration.

It means God be with us…
and may we meet again.

The Making of a Man

Family has always meant a great deal to all of us, especially to my father, who never had a family growing up.

My father was born in Seraye, Eritrea, in 1934. His father died shortly after his birth, and soon after that, his mother grew sick. She could not care for him.

So while still a child, my father moved to a monastery, where he lived with Coptic Christian monks and learned ancient verse and *Giiz* chants from millennia past. And then, at age nine, he left the monastery and wandered to the home of a relative.

Some would say that he lived with his relative, but he might say that he almost died. For living implies life and vitality, and he had neither. He became an unpaid laborer, a servant, an orphan among family.

He started to wonder. *DOES GOD HATE ME? DID HE CURSE ME BEFORE BIRTH? IS THAT WHY FATHER DIED AND MOTHER GOES TO JOIN HIM?*

One day his relative hurled the wooden coffee-grinder at his head. She promised to do much worse, and he feared to stay.

But he could not return to the monastery, and he could not return to his mother, who was still sick. So at age 14, Haileab turned from his homeland of Eritrea and wandered deeper into the heart of Ethiopia, into the province of Tigray.

Alone and almost penniless, he had to rely on strangers as he traveled from small town to small town.

But our people are generous and big of heart, especially among the village folk, and few go hungry while there is any to spare. So he survived.

He arrived finally at the big city they call Mekele, where he found his one rich uncle and many other Eritreans.

Even with support from his uncle and countrymen, though, he sometimes went two or three days without eating. Then he would devour six or seven *injeras* at one sitting. *IT WAS A TIME OF EATING LUNCH, NOT KNOWING WHEN YOU WOULD EAT DINNER,* he later told us. *SO WHENEVER I COULD, I ATE MULTIPLE MEALS IN ONE.*

The monastery and his relative had taught him how to work, so he begged a job at a shanty government clinic, cleaning rooms, folding sheets, making beds.

But he loved drink. He loved women. He loved every vice that a teenage boy loves when he has no adult supervision.

But what one does in youth, one often regrets in old age. *I LIVED A SINFUL LIFE. BUT WHAT WOULD YOU EXPECT? I HAD NO MOTHER, I HAD NO*

FATHER, I HAD NO ONE TO TEACH ME RIGHT OR WRONG. BEJAKOOM, MY CHILDREN, PLEASE DON'T BE LIKE ME.

Despite this weakness, he also worked diligently, cleaning at the clinic. As he cleaned, he listened. As he listened, he lent his hand. And as he lent his hand, he began to learn.

He had learned how to read at the monastery, and now each night, he read whatever books he could get his hands on. Anatomy, physiology, physics, mathematics, chemistry—he learned all the basics of the human body.

One day, all Ethiopian students who dreamed of becoming physicians came to Mekele to take the government's standardized examination. To fail meant a volatile peasant life and dependence on the local economy's unsteady orbit. To pass—as only 5% would—meant a permanent job in the Ethiopian government and a valuable place in society.

Although my father had not attended high school, he took the test with the other students. A vagabond among local favorites, what chance did he have?

He always told the story with pride.

THERE WERE MANY OF US WHO TOOK THE TEST. ONE PERSON SCORED EIGHTY-SIX OUT OF ONE HUNDRED, AND I SCORED EIGHTY-FOUR.

EVERYONE ELSE SCORED BELOW US, SO I EARNED THE RIGHT TO TRAIN AS AN ADVANCED DRESSER. NOT A FULL-FLEDGED DOCTOR, BUT IT DIDN'T MATTER BECAUSE THERE WERE SO FEW DOCTORS THAT AS AN ADVANCED DRESSER, I DID EVERYTHING THAT A FULL DOCTOR DID.

Living in a desperate time, among a desperate people, among wars, among famine, among epidemics, he found that he often held the keys to life.

He also found that books and training were not always enough.

WHAT COULD BOOKS TEACH ME IF I DIDN'T HAVE ACCESS TO THE MEDICAL EQUIPMENT THEY DESCRIBED? WHAT COULD THEY TEACH ME IF I HAD TO TREAT MODERN-DAY HORRORS WITH MIDDLE-AGE TOOLS OR IF I HAD TO TRAVERSE 25 MILES OF BARREN WILDERNESS TO TREAT A BED-RIDDEN MOTHER, KNOWING THAT SHE MIGHT BE DEAD BY THE TIME THAT I ARRIVED?

The decades passed and he became famous among village folks.

Haileab, the son of Zedengel. Birthplace: Seraye, Eritrea. Now living in Tigray, Ethiopia. Deliverer of Babies. Stitcher of the bloody. Mender of the broken.

He would travel any distance. On foot. On mule. At night. By day. In the blistering heat of summer. In the flash floods and deep mud of winter.

One day he would drink 30 cups of *sewa*, or *habesha* beer. The next he would trek six hours to a remote village to save someone's life. One moment he would captivate an entire crowd, pumping his arms to drive home a humorous point. The next he would raise his shoe in anger and rifle it across the room at someone's head.

When did he have his first child? Sixteen? Eighteen? Twenty? I have many half-siblings that I don't know and never will. Most have already departed.

Haileab, the son of Zedengel, rarely cried. But he always cried when he though of his lost children, knowing, perhaps, that he had created his own childhood nightmare in their lives: *YOU CANNOT KNOW HOW IT FEELS TO KNOW THAT YOU BROUGHT CHILDREN INTO THIS WORLD AND ABANDONED THEM. ABANDONED YOUR OWN BLOOD TO THIS HARSH WORLD.*

He married my mother. He was much older than her, maybe 20 years older. But that was the way of our people. A younger man had nothing to offer a woman's parents. He had to accumulate 20 years' wealth to convince the bride-to-be's family that he could provide for the daughter *and* the parents.

Several years after they were married, my brother Tewolde was born, and then me, and then my sister Mehret. All three of us born in Adi Wahla, Ethiopia, not far from the Eritrean border.

All three of us cultural wholes but political half-breeds, with our father from Eritrea and our mother from Ethiopia.

We are the same people. Same language. Same food. Same culture. We even share the same genes. We, the Tigrynia-speaking people.

But somehow, we have formed separate identities, and more recently, have become bitter enemies.

Some say our division started centuries ago.

Many others say it started with the Italians—that when they colonized us in the late 19th century, they separated my father's people from the rest of Ethiopia.

With the end of World War II, the colonizers departed. But they left us to fight through our differences, the differences that they had amplified.

For 30 years, we fought against each other and alongside each other. We took a little break to catch our breath and have resumed fighting now.

Many of my father's and mother's people now hate each other. But they did not hate each other in my father's day. How else could my father, an Eritrean, live among my mother's people for almost three decades? How else could he nurse so many of her people back to life? How else could he marry my mother?

He grew wealthy. He had his own pharmacy, his own general store, and he ran his own clinic. He had livestock by the hundreds and was known to all in the area.

He had many friends, but he also had many enemies. Powerful enemies. They came uninvited and threatened him:

Do not treat this patient. He killed my brother. Didn't you hear me, you son of a woman? I said do not treat him!

You won't stop? OK. Just wait then. I will show you your work. Just wait. We'll see how long your clinic stays open.

My father, a healer, had been robbed of his power to heal. I wonder what he thought....

They have broken into my clinic and destroyed all of my supplies. They have threatened to do worse.

Tigray does not have the medicine that I need, and I fear to go deeper into Ethiopia. My friends warn me not to report to headquarters for more supplies; they say the ruthless Dergue regime will kill or imprison me.

Gathering the provisions that I will need, I pack my mules and head across the border to Sudan. I purchase the supplies—thank God for the black market, I get them for half the price. Let's just pray that these pills are real; even the regular market sells fake pills.

I return and I treat whoever comes to my clinic. Hippocrates lives among us, and I can refuse no sick person.

But my enemies return and even my friends pressure me to choose whom I will treat. Their threats run through my mind all day long:

What? You bought more supplies? You must be crazy. You must not like living.

That time of the month beckons, and I must enter deeper into Ethiopia to report on how many patients I have treated, to receive updated orders, and of course, to receive my monthly salary. But my friends refuse to let me go, telling me to look at my children:

If you want them to grow up fatherless, go ahead and report to headquarters.

I cannot risk it, so I stay. But I keep seeing patients. For I, Haileab, the son of Zedengel, am a doctor. I have served my people for more than 20 years, and I will not stop now.

Good thing that we have savings. Good thing that we planned ahead. We can survive even without my paycheck.

But what use is money if you are not alive? The Dergue approaches with their army. I fear that they will kill me because I did not report to headquarters when I was summoned.

They even say that the Dergue has given their army clearance to wipe out all our people. No questions asked.

Burn and loot. Rape. Create a race of tortured half-breeds who hate at least half of themselves. Annihilate all those who show the slightest resistance.

I have to flee, but what of my family? Can they make it? Can three young children and their mother survive the scorching wilderness? Can I survive it? Can I even flee? Will my friends let me leave? Will my enemies let me leave? Or will they make me join their ranks as an army doctor?

If I flee with my family, all will know what I intend, and they will capture all of us. So I must go alone for now. I will pack my mules slowly and pretend that I go to buy more supplies in Sudan, and then I will stay there.

Do not worry, family. I will get settled and then hire a guide for you.

How will you get through the border and into Sudan? The rebel groups will not let you pass? Yes, this is true, for all of you were born in Ethiopia. Do not fear. I will mail you letters of clearance. The rebels are my friends and will let you through.

Here, too, is money. With money, you can do much.

But exercise great care! Even those who befriend you seek to rob you. Sew the money into your cloth and NEVER take your cloth off. That way, no one can steal it.

I must leave now. My community, my people, my family, my wealth, the status that I have earned through

92

decades of service—I leave all of this behind. I go to join the millions—the refugees in Sudan.

Coffee Tales

As children, Tewolde, Mehret, Hntsa and I knew better than to breach certain topics with our parents. High on the "Never Bring Up" list were boyfriends, girlfriends, and all things sexual. My parents had married by arrangement and considered dating to be a uniquely American *sidinet*, or wickedness, that their children would never practice—at least not while we lived under their roof.

One day, my father grabbed Tewolde and me and sat us down.

DO NOT HAVE SEX. YOU WILL GET AIDS. YOU WILL DIE. YOU WILL HAVE CHILDREN THAT YOU CANNOT SUPPORT. WAIT UNTIL YOU ARE MARRIED.

Conversation over.

My sister Mehret? Hah! One afternoon, poor girl got whooped because she was stranded three miles away at her high school and she accepted a ride home from one of my church friends. My dad was right there to see her get out of the car, and he almost killed her for being alone in a car with a guy. *GESRET! SIDEE! WHO IN YOUR MOTHER'S NAME ARE YOU GOING TO SAY TAUGHT YOU? IF I EVER SEE YOU ALONE IN A CAR WITH A BOY AGAIN, I WILL MAKE YOU LOST!*

Truth be told, the only way we could attend school dances was by appealing to our parents' deep respect for all things educational. We assured them that school dances were highly educational events, that all our classmates attended them, and that we would be left behind if we did not go. Convinced that the dances were vital to our education, our parents let us go—sometimes.

Only one subject was more taboo than sex. It was full of homesickness, displacement, and harsh, harsh separation.

We never asked, sensing the layers of nightmare that asking might uncover.

We always wondered, though. Why had Papa left us in *Adi*? How did we find him again in Sudan? What problems did we encounter on the road? How had we survived?

As we got older, my parents gave us the answers. But as kids, we had only one way of piecing together our past: the coffee tales.

When three or more of my people come together in a home, the woman of the house usually asks the other adults if they want *boona*, or coffee, and they usually say no. Not the least bit fooled, the woman asks again, and the guests usually say yes.

The process of brewing *boona* is different from the American coffee-making process. The woman pours the *boona* beans into a skillet and heats them over a stove, until the powerful aroma of coffee invades the entire house.

Sometimes the cooked beans give off too much smoke, and the smoke detector goes off.

After heating the beans, the woman scoots them into a filter, runs water through, and serves the coffee in small, fragile, white cups, decorated in bright, Oriental designs. The cups are small enough to fit between your fingers, so small that one gulp could empty them. But no one gulps the coffee—everyone sips slowly. The *boona* reaches in and uncuffs their tongues, allowing them to discuss memories they would otherwise leave untouched.

Sometimes, they recount stories of adjustment.

Of Fisoom, who mistook the refrigerator for a clothes dresser. He organized his trousers and shirts on the shelves, even placing his underwear and socks in the pull-out drawers on the bottom.

Of Gebre, who upon arriving at the airport saw a dark-skinned, uniformed airline worker and panicked, thinking that the worker belonged to the Dergue army.

Sometimes, the adults even tell stories of why they left their homeland. Of how a rebel group hunted them, and how they fled across the Red Sea to Saudi Arabia and spent months in a Saudi prison. Of how they somehow made it back across to Port Sudan and then to the States.

The adults in my house would sip slowly and resurrect their pasts. Even my mother. And whenever we could, we kids hid behind the stairs and listened.

When we were in our country, we were doing well. Tewolde, Selamawi, Mehret, they were all born there.

We lived in our own home, with three rooms and a long hall and made of cement—not like many of the other homes. My husband had set up a small clinic and practiced there. We had a pharmacy where we sold pills, penicillin, and soap.

Many village folk came to my husband with malaria; many came with snake bites but died before my husband could treat them; village folks came to my husband on mules and took him back to their villages to help their women give birth.

In those days, many women died as they tried to give birth, and their children died, too.

Sometimes they would bleed to death after they gave birth. Village folks did not understand, they would let the women bleed. But my husband would come and lift their legs up—not too much, just a little bit—and tilt their heads back and let them sleep in this position, so that they would not bleed to death. He would inject them with painkiller, too, and then he would give them light food.

My husband treated everyone. Some came almost dead from stone fights, some had hurt themselves as they watched their livestock, some came wounded from the war. No one taught him how to treat all of their different sicknesses, but he had a great ability to figure out what to do.

After a while, though, there came a time without peace; a time of leaving your home and fleeing, of leaving your children and fleeing; a time when a husband would flee, leaving his wife; a time when all fled, leaving their possessions.

In that time, the Ethiopian dictator Mengistu Haile Mariam and his Dergue regime waged war against the Woyane rebel group and the Jebha rebel group. Sometimes the Jebha and the Woyane waged war against each other.

When the Woyane or Jebha were said to have taken a village, the Dergue would come and try to take it back. When the Dergue came, the people fled, or hid in their homes, or sent their children to the countryside, for they did not want to be caught between the Woyane, the Jebha and the Dergue.

Mengistu's decree, "Ye-matfat Zemacha," struck fear in our hearts. "Kill all living creatures, spare none."

Whenever the armies approached, my husband fled to the wilderness and hid there for several days. He feared that they would take him away, maybe kill him, maybe make him join their ranks as a doctor. One day it became too much—they approached and he fled to Sudan.

We did not know if we would see him again; it was only the will of God that kept us all alive and brought us back together.

All the villagers mourned when he left, the whole territory did, because he had never refused them and he had not feared to put himself in danger when treating them. They wept, saying, "How will we find another like him, like Haileab, the son of Zedengel?"

Some time passed, and my husband had travelers bring us messages: "Come, come, come. What are you waiting for? Come to Sudan, leave the livestock, leave the house, leave everything. Just bring the children and come."

But how could I leave my people and my home?

Dergue kept coming in and out of our village, and we started to fear that Dergue and Woyane would clash in our region.

More and more of our people started to hide in the wilderness, and one time I sent Tewolde and Selamawi to their uncle Nigusay in the village they call Geza Gono. I kept Mehret with me.

Uncle Nigusay came back several days later and told me that he would never again take them. He told me that Selamawi and his cousin, Uncle Nigusay's daughter, were sleeping near the doorway on a bedding that Uncle had set up for them, and that while they slept, a snake came in from outside and started to slither onto Selamawi's body.

"We could do nothing," he said. "We could have hit the snake, but then the snake might have killed Selamawi. We could have warned Selamawi, but Selamawi might have moved

in fear and caused the snake to bite him. So all we could do was watch and pray.

"*The snake moved slowly, from Selamawi's body to my daughter's body, and we kept watching, praying, able to do nothing, until finally the snake slithered past them.*

"*Once we had killed the snake, I raised my voice and my hands to God, and looking up, begged, 'Savior of the world, please save me from breaking the trust that has been given me. Please spare these children's lives and let me bring them back to their mother safely.'*"

So Uncle Nigusay brought Tewolde and Selamawi back to me. He told me, "You gave your children to me that they would be saved, but they almost died with me. From now on, do not hide the children away by themselves. Keep them with you, for who knows where safety lies these days?"

But the sickness they call niphoyoo seized Selamawi, and he almost died. We did not know what to do, and then I said, "Father of Mine, Father of Mine, I will go to Sudan. I won't say I'm tired, or that there are thorns, or that there is cold. I will go to Sudan. Just heal him."

God is good, and Selamawi got better, and we fled to Sudan.

We fled, carrying sugar, medicine, a few clothes, a little money. We left our house and our family and we sold our livestock.

At first, we went on our feet. We piled our two small donkeys with food and we rented a camel, and we had guides to help us for part of the way. I walked much of the way, even with the animals. I still have scars on my shoulder from the chafing where I carried Mehret and Selamawi.

We walked only at night because we feared that a plane would bomb us. From the sky, a pilot could not tell the difference between civilians and guerrilla fighters.

Every night, we would hear the hyenas shriek, INGHOOOOY!, and we would fear. The younger hyenas would say, cheecheechacheecheeechaachee, and we would sit up in terror. The foxes would howl, wild boars would yelp, haaah, haaah, haaah, haaah, and snakes would give noise, chee chee chee chee.

The night air entered my children, and all three became sick with the intense killer cold they call tekh-tekh-ta. They would throw up everything they ate; many children died from it.

We arrived at a small town called Deke Dasheem, a place where snakes wiped out many people and rabid dogs killed many others.

I encountered a woman named Hidaat who had a house of eating, and I told her, "Hidaat, please, I have money, just help my children." God bless her, she helped us.

But the tekh-tekh-ta persisted, and many children died all around us. I begged a doctor named Kidane to treat my children, and he gave them penicillin shots, and after seven weeks, we left Deke Dasheem.

But the sickness persisted, until it became very bad, and then we could not find water. We approached a village and begged them to let us into their homes, but they saw us and said, "They have the strong cold, do not let them enter, we do not want our children to die."

But then a strong storm came and it almost swept us away, and they had pity on us and let us into their homes.

After we entered Sudan, we went from place to place and found many habesha that we knew in a land they call Awad, near Aliberia, and they became frightened when they saw us, saying, "Don't you know that your husband is in a region called Hafeer, and that he is very troubled because of you?" So they sent someone immediately to where my husband was.

But there was an influential woman there who said, "No, they cannot stay here with their tekh-tekh-ta cold." But our friends argued with her, saying, "She is our sister, either throw us away with her or hug us with her."

And the woman said, Let her be, then, and we were able to stay. Then my husband came, and our year of separation was over.

We were all very sick, maybe approaching death, but because of my husband, we became better. He injected the medicine into my children's thighs, into their skin, and they became better.

After some time, my husband heard of the Swedish Ministry clinic in Semsem, in a refugee camp called Umsagata. He went to work there, and I helped at the food and nutrition place, and we lived there for three or so years in our adobe. And then we came to America, and you know the rest.

The Unmaking of a Man

"One day, upon awakening from troubled dreams, Gregor Samsa found himself, in his bed, transformed into a monstrous vermin."

Franz Kafka, *The Metamorphosis*

One day, upon awakening, Haileab Asgedom found himself, in America, transformed into a monstrous black beetle.

He had been an advanced dresser back home in Adi and had done everything: stitching head wounds, birthing babies, treating snakebite and malaria.

But when he came to the States, he couldn't just roll down to Central DuPage Hospital and proclaim, *"Y'ALL ARE IN LUCK. GUESS WHO JUST MOVED INTO YOUR COUNTY—THAT'S RIGHT, THE BADDEST ALL-PURPOSE STITCHER AND BABY-BIRTHER THAT THE BACKWOODS OF TIGRAY EVER DID SEE. JUST SHOW ME THE SURGERY WING, AND I'LL GIVE YOU A FREE DEMONSTRATION."*

No, my father was fortunate to get a job as a janitor at Wheaton College. He worked there for a few months, and then his eyes started to give up. He blamed the bright glare of the snow, but I always thought it had more to do with his glaucoma and the cataracts in his eyes.

His eyesight departed slowly, and his work errors multiplied—a key lost here, a door unlocked there—until his employers had no choice.

He arrived at work one day as Haileab Asgedom, the working man supporting his family.

He returned home that same day as Haileab Asgedom, the unemployed beetle.

Such is the fate of many immigrant fathers, especially those from third-world countries. Those who can find work often toil at menial jobs. Those who cannot, stay home.

For both, life is a far cry from the glory and self-worth they knew back in their homeland.

For Haileab, it meant several levels of dependence.

He could not get a driver's license because he could not pass the vision test. And though he could still ride his bike, he usually relied on others to get around.

On the worst days, his eyes swelled almost completely shut. Then he was forced to stay upstairs in bed.

The doctors could heal him, he told us, if they really wanted to.

WITH ALL OF THEIR EDUCATION AND TECHNOLOGY, THESE DOCTORS COULD HELP ME.

BUT THEY DON'T CARE ABOUT HELPING YOU IN THIS COUNTRY. THE DOCTORS HERE ARE NOT

HOW WE WERE IN ADIENA. THERE, WE TREATED EVERYONE THE BEST THAT WE COULD, REGARDLESS OF THEIR FINANCIAL SITUATION.

BUT IN THIS COUNTRY, THEY CARE ABOUT YOUR MONEY. IF YOU DON'T HAVE MONEY, THEY WON'T GIVE YOU THE REAL TREATMENT BECAUSE THEY ARE NOT ALLOWED TO.

Eventually, my father lost his teeth and had to get dentures. Then came diabetes, which forced him to adjust his diet.

As his physical condition worsened, so did his emotional state. The more time he spent in the house, the more obsessed he became with household details. *SIT DOWN, EVERYONE. WE NEED TO IDENTIFY THE PERSON WHO LEFT THE CUP ON THE STAIRWELL. YOU SHALL NOT MOVE EVEN ONE INCH UNTIL WE FIND THE CULPRIT.*

The most innocent actions became an assault on his character.

CAN YOU BELIEVE THAT FRIEND OF TEWOLDE'S? HOW DARE HE CALL TEWOLDE AND INVITE OUR FAMILY TO DINNER, WITHOUT ASKING ME FIRST?

I GUESS THAT'S WHAT HAPPENS WHEN YOU ARE A FALLEN OAK. NO ONE RESPECTS YOU ANYMORE.

Fearing that he was losing control and respect, he became increasingly paranoid. But what would you expect? He stayed home twenty-four hours a day, unable to work, barely able to see, and dependent on others for his welfare. He had all the time in the world to wish for his past, ponder his present, and question his future.

Still, my father had never known shyness. And he maintained his vigor.

So he focused his energies elsewhere: on his homeland, on his neighborhood, on his family—though not always to our liking.

When we kids were in elementary school, he started to wake us up at five in the morning so we could do aerobics.

WHERE ARE YOU GOING TO SAY THAT YOU GREW UP? EH? HOW ARE YOU GOING TO SAY THAT YOU GREW UP IN WHEATON WHEN YOU DIDN'T TAKE ADVANTAGE OF ALL OF THE RESOURCES THAT YOU HAD AROUND YOU? DO YOU KNOW WHAT THOSE BACK IN ADI WOULD DO TO BE IN YOUR SHOES? ANYTHING.

We wanted to respond with some common sense – *We'll happily say that we grew up in Wheaton, and like everyone else in Wheaton, we want to be asleep right now.*

But that would have resulted in a near-death experience, so we did the aerobics.

Other times, he led us to the Wheaton College track. We usually beat the dawn.

IT IS IMPORTANT FOR YOU TO RUN EVERY DAY AND TO GET STRONG. YOU SEE THE LANES. THERE ARE EIGHT OF THEM. I WANT YOU TO CIRCLE THE TRACK IN EACH OF THOSE LANES ONCE.

Like with the aerobics, we would have mutinied had we not harbored such respect for our good friend *Mr. Quul-fee*. *Mr. Quul-fee* was long and made of animal leather—he could usually be found around my father's waist—and when he came to call, you cried.

So we circled the lanes as fast as we could, racing each other, with my father timing each lap.

But he did not just sit by and time us; he practiced what he preached. No matter how much his 50-year-old frame ached, he always hobbled the two miles with us. He would walk part of it, if necessary, but he always finished all eight laps.

YOU SEE, I AM NOT ASKING YOU TO DO SOMETHING THAT I WOULD NOT DO MYSELF.

He pressed on. Before school, after school, on the weekends, at night, he never rested.

YOU NEED TO GET USED TO WORKING HARD, SO WE ARE GOING TO CLEAN THE WHOLE HOUSE TONIGHT. WATCH ME AS I SWEEP AND MOP. WHEN I MOP, NOTICE THAT THE FIRST TIME THROUGH, I DO A PURE WATER MOP TO GET ALL OF THE DIRT OFF, AND THEN AFTER THAT, I MOP EVERYTHING AGAIN WITH DISINFECTANT.

SELAMAWI, WHY ARE YOU PUSHING SO HARD WITH THE BROOM? YOU ARE SCATTERING THE DUST EVERYWHERE. I WONDER SOMETIMES: WHO ARE YOU GOING TO SAY TAUGHT YOU LATER ON WHEN PEOPLE SEE YOU SWEEPING?

We learned how to sweep, mop, dust. We even learned how to make beds hospital-style, and after that, we were put to work outside.

Among other tasks, we had to rake the long driveway that we shared with our neighbors. By the time we had finished clearing the leaves, we would look back to where we had begun and see a new collection of leaves building up. We would start again, going even faster, praying that we could beat the leaves and rush inside before they piled up again.

Babay, why are you making us do this? Our neighbors don't even care, and none of their kids have to do it.

LISTEN TO ME, MY CHILDREN. IT IS PAINFUL FOR YOU NOW, BUT BELIEVE ME, THE DAY WILL COME WHEN YOU WILL THANK ME. FOR I AM TEACHING YOU HOW TO WORK AND HOW TO LIVE WELL WITH YOUR NEIGHBORS.

THE DAY COMES IN EACH OF OUR LIVES WHEN THOSE AROUND US ARE ASKED TO TESTIFY AND TO TELL WHAT KIND OF CHARACTER WE HAVE DEMONSTRATED IN OUR PAST.

I guess my father knew what he was talking about. When I was in eighth grade, our landlord raised the rent and we were evicted from our home on College Avenue. It looked like we would have to leave Wheaton.

But the folks at the Marian Park housing development moved us up several years on the waiting list. Before they could do us this special favor, though, they had to ask our neighbors on College Avenue what kind of people we were. The day of character examination had come!

Our wonderful neighbors, Linda Panther, Linda Slinger, and Peggy Hackett, said good things about us, and we moved to Marian Park.

Not too long after we moved, my father decided to rake the many leaves next to Marian Park's lake. This time, his desire to help his neighbors would get him in trouble.

None of us kids were around, so my father tried to clean the entire lakefront by himself. He raked and raked and raked until the day had departed and evening had dawned. He finally finished raking and gathered the leaves into a huge, light-brown mountain.

Then he got his big boots. Wading into the water, circling slowly, gathering litter, debris, and fallen branches as he went, he cleaned Marian Park's lake. By the time he finished, night had arrived and he had encountered his first major problem.

He had created the mountain of leaves, litter, and sticks, but he could not figure out how to get rid of it. The mountain dwarfed the nearby dumpster, so he could not throw away the leaves.

He came up with a plan: He would burn the leaves down to nothing. He had started and managed many fires back in *Adi*, so keeping this one under control would pose no challenge.

He started the fire and watched the leaves burn slowly.

Suddenly, he heard sirens. Firemen rushed to extinguish my father's blaze, and a policeman ran toward him.

My father could not have been more confused.

X CUES ME. I RAKE AND TRY TO FIX LEAVES. X CUES ME. I DO NOT UNDERSTAND. NO, I AM POOR MAN, I AM DISABILITY. PLEASE, DO NOT TAKE ME TO THE HOUSE OF IMPRISONMENT. PLEASE DO NOT STAIN MY RECORD.

The firemen had arrived so quickly because there was a fire station across from the main Marian Park entrance. They were stunned by my father's explanation: that he thought he could start a huge fire in the middle of private property.

The law compelled the officers to arrest or at least fine him. But after talking to him, they instead obeyed the Golden Rule and gave him only a warning.

YOU SEE HOW THIS TREACHEROUS WORLD WORKS? SOMETIMES YOU TRY TO DO SOMETHING GOOD AND YOU END UP GETTING PUNISHED FOR IT.

Although we *habesha* refugees have scattered to every imaginable corner of the Earth, we occasionally gather by the hundreds at old banquet halls in Chicago.

At each get-together, we come yearning for fellowship. We also search for news of the homeland, something we desperately sought before 1991, when the civil war between Eritrea and Ethiopia still raged fiercely.

In the earliest days, at our very first party, the Chicago *habesha* kids jumped Tewolde and me in the hallway within minutes of our arrival. They had their own little gang.

"You suburban commandos, we're gonna beat your butt!"

Tewolde and I ran into the closet, reappeared with brooms and started swinging at the city boys, wild as we could.

Believe it or not, we became friends in later years.

We usually hung out in the hallways of the old buildings. When we grew tired, we would retreat to the main room and sit at a table with our other young friends. The adults would sit at their own tables, the women usually at different tables from the men.

The dancing began around 11 p.m. and did not finish until 4 or 5 a.m. Before the dancing, though, they always had announcements, news-sharing and other pre-planned programs.

My father would interrupt the programs, rising and leaving his seat, heading right for the stage. He would take the microphone and start reciting *geetmes*, or rhyming poems.

Being a child, I would cringe in embarrassment. "Who is that?" they would ask, especially the kids who lived in

Chicago and did not know that he was my father. "Does anyone know where that crazy old man came from?"

I kept my mouth shut, denying him, too ashamed to acknowledge him.

He had a rare talent for rhyming in *geetme*, our culture's spoken-word freestyle rap. He would go on for half an hour without pause.

"ISIKOOM DHO KITBAHALOO AKAHL GODOLO, AYNISIKUM INDEEKUM BEHAGOS NETEE MULUO KEYHEE BAHREE TIZELILWO."

"OH, YOU, WHO ARE CALLED HANDICAPPED. AREN'T YOU THE VERY ONES WHO WITH BOUNDLESS JOY LEAP OVER THE EXPANSIVE RED SEA?"

All listened in amazement, wondering, who was this eccentric old man? Did he not fear to interrupt the program? Did he not realize that shouting into a microphone creates sonic hell? And how was it that he loved his homeland so much that he could sing-say half-hour *geetmes* about it?

Some days he would write the lyrics ahead of time. But then his eyes would fail him and he would struggle to read his own writing, even when he held the paper right up to his bifocals.

He would call my friend Abraham, who was my age but had come to this country later and could still read Tigrynia quickly.

ABRAHAM, MY SON, ARE YOU HERE? PLEASE COME AND READ THIS FOR ME. Abraham would go up respectfully and read the rhymes, with my father's hunched frame standing guard next to him.

In my younger days, my embarrassment created a smokescreen that blocked me from hearing my father's rhymes. But as I got older, maturity opened my ears and my heart, and the haze thinned. I started to feel his words and the spirit beneath them, and then, I started recognizing his genius.

I remember one time when his poetry rivaled Homer, Virgil, and Shakespeare. I waited until we got home and then asked him to repeat the lines.

I have since forgotten those lines, but I can never forget the quiet, almost embarrassed shock that flooded his eyes when I asked him to repeat them. It was the shock of a man who had slowly been convinced by those around him that he had little to offer; a man whose new country had labeled him insignificant; a man whose opinion rarely mattered as it once had.

It was the shock of a proud man who had metamorphosed into a beetle.

Several years later, I ran into an old friend named Berhe at an annual Eritrean conference in Columbus, Ohio. I had met him when I was a boy—each year, he had helped drive my family to the conference.

My family hadn't attended one of the conferences in a few years. But the summer after my freshman year in college, I decided to go alone.

Berhe was thrilled to see me. He grabbed me and hugged me three times and pelted me with questions.

How are you doing? How is your family? Your health? School? Your family? How are your parents and siblings? School? Your family? And you? How is your health? Mother? Father? And you? How are you?

Dehaan, I repeated, *we are fine. Dehaan, dehaan, dehaan.*

I sat with Berhe and talked of old times. We laughed as we remembered stories of going to the camp together. He told me of his wife and kids, and I congratulated him.

Then Berhe started to tell me stories about my father.

Sima, Selamawi, he began. *Listen.*

I went back to the homeland recently and ran into some of your father's old friends in Tigray. Old-timers, dinosaurs from way back in the day. There are only a few of them left now—thirty years of war made sure of that.

The old-timers started to tell me stories of Haileab, the son of Zedengel, stories of the deeds that he had done and the people that he had helped. We sat in the tavern, and the tavern filled up, and more and more came. Many others, even younger ones, started to speak of him:

"He walked through miles of winter mud to help my aunt give birth."

"He saved my grandfather from the snakebite's certain death."

"He stitched my head up after the son of Tesfi busted it open with a stone."

"He always gave what he could to the poor, even giving them animals during feast times so that they would not go hungry."

"His generosity knew no bounds. How we mourned when they came for him and he fled. For who was ever like him, like Haileab, our father and our friend."

As I listened to all of these witnesses testify to your father's love and his heart, I became overwhelmed with emotion. All of them regarded your father as a true hero. A generous, talented hero who served his people with great love and distinction.

I am glad that you and I were made to find each other today so that I could tell you all of these things. In my heart, I knew that it was you and your siblings who should have heard those stories, not me.

All throughout my childhood, I had witnessed my father's metamorphosis. Watching him deteriorate, seeing him dependent on others, feeling sorry for him and even feeling embarrassed, I had witnessed his unmanning.

All that time, the thought had never occurred to me that my father had once been a hero. Or that he might *still* be a hero, tragic and flawed though he might be.

Eyeing the Mountaintop

Growing up, I saw my parents welcome many guests into our home. It didn't matter who the person was or how much they had. The poorest, most recently arrived refugee received the same welcome as the richest American. *Sit down, please. Have some injera. Have something to drink.*

I used to think that the whole world shared my parents' philosophy. As I grew older, though, my eyes opened.

I saw that most people used a different calculator. Beauty was external, money mattered, and so did skin color. I looked some more and saw that those who discriminated most, those who saw angels only when angels could help them, were often the ones who had the most.

And I thought to myself, this seeing angels thing, maybe it offers only spiritual rewards. Maybe God will reward us in another land someday. Maybe the reward is in our hearts and in the kind of people we become.

I was convinced, though, that the reward was not a material one.

But that was fine with me. Especially after my brother passed away. I had watched him see angels in the least likely places, and wanted nothing more than to be like him.

So I did my best to follow in his and my parents' footsteps.

I never could have imagined where those footsteps would lead me.

After my brother died, the mantle of the oldest passed to me. I knew that I had to take responsibility for my family. I also knew that academic success would help me to help them.

Even before Tewolde died, though, I had always approached my schoolwork with the highest dedication. Starting in elementary school, I read books in my room until my father screamed at me to come out: *YOU! HOW LONG ARE YOU GOING TO SIT IN THERE BY YOURSELF? IF YOU DO NOT LEARN TO MINGLE WITH PEOPLE, YOU WILL BECOME LIKE THOSE WILD ONES WHO NEVER SPEAK WITH ANYONE.*

But I kept reading. I read thousands of pages a week and cleared out whole sections of the Wheaton Public Library. The Hardy Boys. Encyclopedia Brown. And my favorite, Alfred Hitchcock's Three Investigators.

Then I started on the biographies in the children's section: Knute Rockne, Martin Luther King, and many others.

As I read, my English improved dramatically. I graduated from Longfellow's ESL (English as a Second Language) program at the end of second grade, and by sixth grade, I was making the high honor roll.

By then, though, some of my classmates had discovered the best way to hurt me—not with their fists, but with their words: *Your father doesn't even work, does he? How come you wore that shirt again? Nerd! Why you so poor?*

I started to see through that dangerous lie that all kids are taught: "Stick and stones can break your bones, but words can never hurt you."

Sticks and stones can indeed break our bones, but words can often do worse. They can stifle, destroy and mutilate all of the beautiful, hopeful things inside of us.

My middle-school classmates massacred my self-esteem. My grades dropped. I got my first 'D' in eighth grade and started to wonder if I could make it academically. High school was fast approaching, and I feared that it might chew me up and spit me out.

But the good thing about words is that they can also breathe life into our spirits. My brother and family encouraged me: *Don't give up. You're smart enough. All you have to do is work hard and believe.*

My faith in God gave me confidence. And as I entered high school, I set my sights on the scholarship my parents had hoped for.

I chose the hardest freshman schedule possible: Advanced Geometry, Advanced English, Advanced Biology.

But there was one advanced class that I couldn't take: Advanced World History. I wanted to take it, but there were only 20 spots available for our class of 400.

Our performance on a middle-school test determined whether we could take the class. The test was loaded with absurd, abstract questions, such as: "If you were on Mars and you came across a stream of liquid that you had never seen before, whom would you ask to help you cross it: a) A Psychologist; b) A Mechanic; c) A Nurse; d) None of the above."

I had never visited Mars; I didn't make the cut.

So I enrolled in Intermediate World History with 200 other freshmen. I knew what I had to do to earn a spot in the advanced sophomore history class.

I scored the highest grade out of all 200 students, setting the class' curve both semesters.

After the year ended, I asked my World History teacher and my counselor to move me up to the advanced class. They agreed.

Still, I wasn't sure how I would fare. Advanced U.S. History was one of the toughest classes in the school.

A part of me wondered, too, if that placement test in middle school had been right. Maybe these white kids really were smarter than me. Maybe I couldn't keep up with them.

Advanced U.S. History would reveal the truth.

Using the bench in my room as my desk, I stayed up night after night, re-reading the chapters and reviewing my notes.

I would get home from sports at 6 p.m., eat, help out around the house, and study until midnight. Then I would get up at 6 a.m. and do it all over again.

The hard work paid off. I often got the highest grade in the class, and I carried an 'A' through the entire first semester.

I was getting straight 'A's in all of my classes. And then the drunk driver killed Tewolde.

And then everything fell apart.

I kept asking myself: How could something this beautiful be stolen by someone else's recklessness? If that's what life was like, then what were we striving for, anyway?

Giving up seemed like a good option. But I loved my family too much. And I remembered Tewolde. He wasn't the kind of brother that ever gave up.

So I turned to God for strength and pushed myself even harder. I aced my finals and maintained my straight 'A's.

During the second semester, I earned straight 'A's again. Sometimes I took extreme measures to get the grade that I wanted, as in my junior English class.

Tewolde had warned me about the teacher: "She doesn't give 'A's."

Still, I came close. I needed a 96 on the final to get an 'A' in the class. But that was pretty much impossible—her tests were nightmares.

There was only one way I could ace the final: Re-read every book that we had covered. Take notes and have them fresh in my mind.

So I did it. Over Christmas vacation, I read and took notes on more than 1,200 pages.

I couldn't finish every book, though; I didn't have time to re-read *Ethan Frome*. So I went to sleep the night before, praying that Ethan Frome would mind his own business and stay off my exam.

A snowstorm hit the next morning, forcing our school to shut down. I stayed home and re-read *Ethan Frome*.

The test was as hard as I thought it would be. But I had every book fresh in my mind, and I aced it. And I aced the class.

While schoolwork consumed most of my energy, I still loved basketball. I was thrilled when I made the freshman team.

But being on the team had its own challenges.

Often, especially on Saturdays, I couldn't get a ride to practice. So I would run the three miles. On the coldest days, I showed up unable to dribble because my hands had become icicles. And on a few crazy days, I ran to practice, ran all throughout practice, then ran back home.

After the season ended, I decided to focus completely on schoolwork. I hadn't planned on joining the track team.

But one day after school, my basketball coach, Coach Kroger, saw me getting on the bus. It's funny how one word of encouragement can change your life.

"What are you doing going home, Mawi? You should be on the track team—you were always way up there in the wind sprints."

Several weeks later, I ran in my first meet. By the end of the season, I was among the fastest freshmen in our conference.

I wanted good running shoes, but spending $50 on a new pair was out of the question. So I wore a raggedy pair that my mom had rustled up. My track coach, Jim Martin, noticed almost immediately.

For each of the next four years, he paid for my training shoes and racing spikes. Sometimes he even took me shopping for school clothes—without telling anyone.

Even with such support from my coach, I made only marginal progress during my sophomore and junior years.

So at the end of my junior year, I made myself a promise: That summer, I would run at least six days a week and lift weights every other day.

I did it, working during the day and training at night.

The hard work paid big dividends. In cross country, where four schools in our conference were ranked among the state's top 20, I earned all-conference honors.

Fueled by my improvement in cross-country season, I kept training during the brutal Illinois winter. I ran almost 400 outdoor miles between November and January and lifted weights in my room every other day. Before I went to sleep each night, I recorded my mileage and weight training at the front of my journal.

The discipline paid off again. In track, I ran the anchor leg on our all-state 4 x 800-meter relay team. We won our conference championship and competed in the state finals.

Looking back at the great memories, I'm always thankful that Coach Kroger stopped me alongside that bus my freshman year.

I was never one of the popular kids in high school, but during my sophomore year, I finally started to develop close friendships: some with kids on my sports teams, some with kids from the advanced-level classes. And I still had my refugee brothers and sisters from back in the day.

No matter whom I hung out with, I always tried not to view my classmates through the caste system that runs most high schools: the cool kids—usually beautiful kids or athletes; the normal kids—who comprise most of the school; and the dreaded ones—the nerds.

Most of my friends were from the lower two castes. But that was fine. My parents and my brother had taught me to see beauty in everyone. And to be honest, I often saw the least beauty in the coolest, most popular kids.

It's funny how things work out. My best non-*habesha* friend in high school was Mike Olander—the same kid from whom my brother and I had "borrowed" all those Reese's so many Halloweens ago.

Mike ran track and cross country with me and went out of his way to give me rides to school. One day, in September of our senior year, he picked me up at 6:30 a.m. for our first National Honor Society meeting.

About 60 of our classmates had gathered in the auditorium. We were late. I grabbed a seat next to Bonnie Nadzam, the girl that I and every other guy had a crush on.

An announcement went out: "Last Call for Nominations for President." I thought for a second about raising my hand. I had never participated in student government, partly because I couldn't get rides to the early meetings and partly because I wasn't popular enough to get elected.

But I figured, what the heck? So I asked Mike to nominate me.

I didn't think I had much of a chance. Six or seven other students were running, many much cooler than me.

We closed our eyes and voted. We opened them again, and I was the president.

I looked around the room, and I knew what had happened. Half of my classmates had voted for a cool kid. But there had been three or four to choose from, so none of them could amass many votes.

The other half of the class wouldn't have voted for the cool kids if their lives had depended on it. Why? Because all throughout high school, the cool kids had made them feel like beetles.

I hadn't. And that's how I got elected. I had treated everyone as an angel.

I wasn't the first person in my family to apply to college. Tewolde had started to apply. He had an 'A' average and good test scores, and he would have had fantastic letters of recommendation—every teacher loved him. But he never finished the application process.

Like him, I wanted to stay close to home, and when my senior year started, I pretty much knew where I wanted to go: Taylor University in Indiana. I had just gone through their summer honors program, and it had sold me on the school.

The only real question was how I would pay for it.

I remember visiting my counselor, Mrs. Martin, to get some tips. She was my track coach's wife, and she had also been my coach for scholastic bowl.

I've said it before, and I'll say it again: It's funny what a few words of encouragement can do. She told me that I could probably go to school anywhere I wanted. Duke, Yale, maybe even Harvard.

I thought she was crazy. *Mrs. Martin,* I wanted to shout, *I'm about the most ghetto, poor, welfare, refugee brother that ever lived. Those schools are gonna laugh if they get an application from someone like me.*

But she kept encouraging me to apply. "Let the admissions committees say no," she told me. "Don't say no for them. You're ranked in the top one percent of your class. You have top test scores. You never know, they might just say yes."

Then Mike's mom, who had become a second mother to me, started to encourage me. Then several of my teachers pitched in.

So I decided to do it. I found out what achievement tests those schools required and took them in December— long after most applicants had taken them and right before each school's application was due.

Then I got my letters of recommendation. Later, when I talked to college administrators, they told me that the letters of recommendation had made the biggest impact.

What had those letters been about? They had said little about my grades but much about my attitude. Seeing beauty in others had paid off again.

In fact, seeing angels had helped even with my grades. My transcript included several 'A's that could have been 'B's. But those teachers had appreciated how I treated my classmates, and they had also appreciated my work ethic, so they had bumped me up to the 'A.'

I applied to eight schools in all: Taylor, Miami of Ohio, Illinois, Duke, Wake Forest, Washington U. in St. Louis, Yale, and Harvard. I applied to so many because I didn't know if any would give me a scholarship.

The only problem with this strategy was that each application cost about $50. I got some schools to waive the application fee. For the rest, I attached a letter to my application, explaining that I could not afford the fee and asking if they would please consider my application, anyway.

They did.

First, I heard from Miami of Ohio. They flew me to their campus and offered me a sizable merit scholarship.

Then Duke flew me out. They offered even more.

Last came Wash. U. They flew me out for a four-day weekend and offered a merit scholarship worth $90,000—free tuition, plus an annual stipend.

I got home and found two envelopes waiting for me, one from Harvard and the other from Yale.

I opened them and read their contents. Then I walked over to the living room to tell my parents. Their dream had come true. Their boy had earned admission to the best universities in the country.

And Harvard—the best-known one in the land—had offered him a full-tuition scholarship.

Father Haileab

During the last two years of my father's life, I only saw him for about four weeks. We spent two weeks together in December of 1997, during Christmas Break of my junior year at Harvard. After that, I never saw him again.

During those last two weeks, we sat together on the beaten-up, dirt-brown couches that we had bought back in 1992. These couches were the first ones we had ever bought; all our others had come from our free mall or our friends.

But this had been a special occasion. My mother, after 12 years of homesickness, had gone back to *Adi* to see her mother and family. My father, declaring that we had to do something for her, had gone down to the Indian brother that all *habeshas* went to back then and bargained for the couches on the eve of her return.

We sat on those sagging couches almost six years later, and my father started telling Hntsa and me stories that we had never heard before:

"ONE TIME, WHEN WE HAD JUST COME TO THIS COUNTRY AND OUR HABESHA BROTHERS AND SISTERS HAD JUST STARTED TO TRICKLE IN, TEMESGEN AND KIBROM CALLED ME TO HELP THEM."

Temesgen and Kibrom were two skin-and-bones brothers, not even 20 when they first came to the States. They had lived with us for several weeks until their sponsors had found them a home.

"THEY HAD GOTTEN THEMSELVES INTO TROUBLE AND DID NOT KNOW ANY ENGLISH. KNOWING NO ONE ELSE WHO COULD TRANSLATE FOR THEM, THEY CALLED ME.

I HAD WARNED TEMESGEN BEFORE THAT AMERICA IS NOT LIKE ADI. I HAD WARNED HIM THAT THIS IS A COUNTRY WHERE YOU CAN BE JUST ONE PENNY SHORT AT THE GROCERY STORE, AND THEY STILL WON'T FORGIVE YOU.

BUT YOU KNOW TEMESGEN, HE HAS NEVER CONSIDERED THE TALK OF PEOPLE.

THEY WERE DRIVING ONE DAY NEAR THE RAILROAD TRACKS, WHEN TEMESGEN BECAME DISTRACTED BY SOMETHING ON THE SIDE OF THE ROAD.

THE NEXT THING HE KNEW, HIS CAR HAD JOLTED OVER THE CURB AND BROKEN THROUGH SEVERAL SIGNS, HALTING ONLY AFTER IT HAD DEMOLISHED A YOUNG PLANT.

HOPING TO ESCAPE BEFORE ANY AUTHORITIES ARRIVED, TEMESGEN AND KIBROM FRANTICALLY

TRIED TO GET THE CAR STARTED. BUT A POLICEMAN CHANCED UPON THEM ALMOST IMMEDIATELY. HE ACCUSED THEM OF DRIVING WITHOUT RULE, BREAKING THE CITY SIGNS, AND KILLING THE YOUNG PLANT.

THEY CAME AND BEGGED ME, 'PLEASE, FATHER HAILEAB! HELP US! THEY HAVE THREATENED TO TAKE AWAY TEMESGEN'S LICENSE AND TO MAKE US PAY FOR THE DAMAGED PROPERTY. THEY WILL STAIN OUR RECORDS AND MAKE US LOST!'

I DID NOT KNOW WHAT TO DO OR HOW I COULD HELP THEM, BUT I AGREED TO GO TO COURT WITH THEM SO THAT I COULD AT LEAST TRANSLATE ON THEIR BEHALF."

Hntsa and I looked at each other with excitement, trying to imagine our father before a judge. This was going to be better than the "Sanford and Son" episode where Fred G. Sanford went to defend his son Lamont and got charged with contempt of court!

WE WENT TO COURT, AND THE JUDGE ASKED ME IF I KNEW ENOUGH ENGLISH TO TRANSLATE AND IF I UNDERSTOOD BOTH LANGUAGES. I TOLD HIM YES AND I TOOK THE PROMISE THAT THEY MAKE YOU TAKE IN COURT.

THE JUDGE ASKED ME TO ASK THEM IF THEY WERE GUILTY OF DESTROYING THE PLANTS AND THE SIGNS. I WAS GOING TO SAY YES. BUT I HAVE PSYCHOLOGICAL KNOWLEDGE—KNOWLEDGE THAT IS NOT CONTAINED IN BOOKS—SO I STOPPED MYSELF. I KNEW THAT IF WE SAID YES, THE JUDGE WOULD FINE THEM AND GIVE THEM MANY OTHER PUNISHMENTS.

BUT WE COULD NOT SAY NO, EITHER, BECAUSE THE POLICEMAN WAS RIGHT THERE AND HE HAD SEEN THEM TRYING TO START THE CAR.

'LISTEN TO ME,' I COUNSELED THEM. 'IF YOU SAY NO, HE WILL KNOW THAT YOU ARE LYING AND HE MIGHT GIVE YOU AN EVEN GREATER PUNISHMENT FOR YOUR DISHONESTY. BUT IF YOU SAY YES, HE WILL STILL CONVICT YOU AND YOU WILL STILL FACE GREAT PUNISHMENT BEYOND YOUR MEANS.'

'SO LET'S TELL HIM THAT A CHILD CAME ACROSS YOUR PATH WHEN YOU WERE DRIVING AND YOU HAD TO CHOOSE BETWEEN HARMING THE CHILD AND DESTROYING THE PLANTS AND THE SIGNS. BECAUSE YOU HOLD NOTHING HIGHER THAN THE LIFE OF A CHILD, YOU

PURPOSEFULLY HOPPED OVER THE CURB AND DESTROYED THE PROPERTY.'

'THAT'S EXACTLY WHAT HAPPENED!' THEY BOTH NODDED. 'TELL HIM!'

SO I TOLD THE JUDGE. HE DID NOT UNDERSTAND ME AT FIRST, AND NEITHER DID THE POLICEMAN, BUT I EXPLAINED IT TO HIM IN A GOOD WAY AND HE UNDERSTOOD.

Hntsa and I knew our father well enough to understand what he meant by "a good way." We could picture him hunched over in the courtroom, with his head raised high and his body leaning on his cane, taking a deep breath, starting softly, then raising his voice to a near-shout, hands pumping emphatically to accentuate his points.

X CUES ME, FATHER. WE ARE POOR. YOU SEE ME, I AM DISABILITY. I AM POOR MAN AND REFUGEE.... That poor judge, that poor policeman, that poor courtroom!

'WHY DIDN'T THEY TELL THE POLICEMAN ABOUT THE CHILD?' THE JUDGE ASKED.

'VERY GOOD,' I TOLD HIM. 'THAT IS GOOOOOOOD QUESTION.'

I HAD BEEN EXPECTING HIS QUESTION AND I HAD AN ANSWER READY FOR HIM: THE CHILD'S MOTHER HAD GRABBED HER CHILD AND RUN OFF

BECAUSE SHE WAS SO TERRIFIED. MOTHER AND CHILD HAD VANISHED BEFORE THE POLICEMAN COULD SEE THEM.

AS TO TEMESGEN AND KIBROM EXPLAINING THEMSELVES TO THE POLICEMAN, I TOLD THE JUDGE THAT THEY HAD JUST COME TO THIS COUNTRY AND COULD NOT COMMUNICATE.

I DO NOT LIKE TO LIE—YOU KNOW THAT THE BIBLE ITSELF TELLS US THAT WE SHOULD NOT LIE. BUT THEY CAME TO ME AND ASKED FOR HELP, AND I KNEW ONLY ONE WAY TO HELP THEM.

My father paused before continuing with his next tale.

ANOTHER TIME, THE SON OF TESFU CALLED ME IN A PANIC. HIS FAMILY HAD JUST COME TO THIS COUNTRY AND HAD MOVED INTO THEIR HOME WHEN THEIR YOUNGEST SON, THE BIG, LUMBERING ONE, WENT TO TAKE A BATH.

WELL, HAILOM HAD NEVER TAKEN A BATH THE AMERICAN WAY AND DID NOT KNOW HOW TO OPEN THE WATER. HE PUT HIS BIG, KEKINDE GELE, HANDS ON THE TWO WATER OPENERS, AND INSTEAD OF TURNING THE OPENERS, HE PULLED.

I DON'T NEED TO TELL YOU HOW STRONG HE IS. HE WRENCHED BOTH OPENERS OUT OF THE WALL.

THE WATER STARTED TRICKLING OUT AT FIRST, THEN RUSHED AT HIM IN FIERCER BURSTS. SOON, IT HAD FLOODED THE BATHROOM AND FLOWED TO THE REST OF THE HOUSE.

THE POOR FAMILY SCURRIED LIKE A ROOSTER WITH ITS HEAD CUT OFF, TO THE KITCHEN, TO THE BASEMENT, TO THE LITTLE PIPES OUTSIDE, LOOKING FOR A WAY TO TURN THE WATER OFF. BUT THEY HAD NO IDEA WHAT THEY WERE DOING. THE WATER KEPT CLIMBING HIGHER AND HIGHER, AND DAMAGING MORE AND MORE OF THE TOWNHOUSE, SEEPING INTO THE WALLS AND EVEN INTO THE APPLIANCES.

FINALLY, THE SON OF TESFU KNOCKED FRANTICALLY ON HIS NEIGHBOR'S DOOR. HE COULD NOT TALK WITH HER BECAUSE HE DID NOT KNOW ENGLISH, BUT SHE UNDERSTOOD THAT HE NEEDED HELP, AND SHE RAN BACK WITH HIM AND TURNED OFF THE CENTRAL WATER SOURCE.

BUT IT WAS TOO LATE. THE WATER HAD FLOODED THE ENTIRE HOUSE, AND WORST OF

ALL, IT HAD SEEPED INTO THE WALLS. PERMANENT DAMAGE HAD BEEN DONE.

WHEN THE LANDLORD SAW HIS HOUSE RUINED, HE BECAME CRAZED AND TOOK THEM TO THE HOUSE OF JUDGMENT, CLAIMING SOME THOUSANDS OF DOLLARS. BUT SEVERAL THOUSAND DOLLARS MIGHT AS WELL HAVE BEEN A BILLION DOLLARS—THEY COULDN'T PAY IT.

I HAD ALREADY TRANSLATED FOR THEM DURING THEIR FIRST DAYS, AS I HAD DONE AND STILL DO FOR MANY OF THE HABESHA. THEY HAD HEARD ABOUT HOW I HAD HELPED TEMESGEN AND KIBROM YEARS AGO. SO THEY CAME TO ME AND BEGGED ME FOR HELP. AGAIN, I DID NOT KNOW HOW I COULD HELP, BUT I COULD NOT REFUSE THEM.

I TOLD THE JUDGE—A DIFFERENT JUDGE FROM THE LAST TIME—THAT I COULD TRANSLATE. AGAIN, I TOOK THE PROMISE. AFTER EXPLAINING THE ACCUSATIONS TO ME, THE JUDGE ASKED ME TO ASK THEM IF THEY WERE GUILTY.

LIKE WITH TEMESGEN, I KNEW THAT WE COULD NOT COMPLETELY DENY OUR GUILT. THE PROOF WAS TOO STRONG.

BUT NEITHER COULD WE ADMIT OUR GUILT BECAUSE THEN THEY WOULD PUNISH US BEYOND OUR MEANS.

'WE ARE POOR PEOPLE,' I TOLD THE JUDGE. 'WE DO NOT KNOW YOUR LANGUAGE OR YOUR WAYS, ESPECIALLY WHEN WE FIRST COME HERE. THEY CAME TO THIS COUNTRY FROM THE BACKCOUNTRIES OF ERITREA AND SUDAN, AND THERE, WE DO NOT HAVE PLUMBING SYSTEMS. HERE, YOU CAN EASILY OPEN THE WATER AND TAKE A DRINK OR A BATH. THERE, JUST TO DRINK WATER, YOU MIGHT HAVE TO DRAG THE WATER FROM THE WELL, EMPTY IT INTO A KETTLE, AND BOIL IT TO KILL THE PARASITES.

'WHEN THIS FAMILY CAME HERE, THEY DID NOT KNOW HOW TO OPEN THE WATER. IN FACT, YOU ARE LOOKING AT A FAMILY THAT KNEW SO LITTLE ABOUT LIFE IN AMERICA THAT WHEN THEY CAME, THEY MARKED THE SAME BIRTH DATE FOR THEMSELVES. LOOK AT THEIR MEDICAID CARD HERE; IT SAYS THAT ALL SIX OF THEM WERE BORN ON JANUARY 1.

'THE SON WENT TO THE BATHROOM, HOPING TO TAKE A BATH, AND INSTEAD, HE FLOODED THE

HOUSE. WE DO NOT DENY HIS MISTAKE, AND IT SEEMS THAT HE SHOULD BE PUNISHED.

'BUT LET'S THINK ABOUT THIS: WHO REALLY MADE THE MISTAKE?

'THE LANDLORD KNEW THAT HIS TENANTS WERE REFUGEES FROM AN UNDEVELOPED COUNTRY. HE KNEW THAT THEY HAD JUST ARRIVED. DID HE GIVE THEM A TOUR OF THE HOUSE AND EXPLAIN THE NECESSARY THINGS TO THEM? DID HE EXPLAIN HOW TO TURN THE FIRE ON? DID HE EXPLAIN HOW TO OPEN AND CLOSE THE HEAT? DID HE EXPLAIN HOW TO OPEN AND CLOSE THE WATER?

'WHOSE FAULT IS IT, THEN, FATHER? DOES THE BLAME LIE WITH THESE POOR REFUGEES? IS IT FAIR TO PUNISH THEM FOR BEING UNFAMILIAR WITH THEIR NEW ENVIRONMENT? IS IT RIGHT TO PUNISH THEM FOR HAVING HAD TO FLEE THEIR HOMELAND AGAINST THEIR WILL?

'OR IS IT FAIR TO BLAME THE LANDLORD, WHO DID NOT TAKE EVEN ONE SECOND TO SHOW THEM HOW TO TAKE CARE OF HIS HOME?

'I THINK THAT THE PATH OF RIGHTNESS IS THAT THE LANDLORD SHOULD BE ON TRIAL RIGHT NOW FOR NOT HONORING THE RULE OF

LANDLORDS. HE SHOULD HAVE TO PAY THEM MONEY FOR ALL OF THE TIME THAT THEY SPENT CLEANING HIS FLOOD AND FOR ALL OF THE ANGUISH THAT THIS EXPERIENCE HAS CAUSED THEM.'

My father leaned back on the couch and smiled.

I'M TELLING YOU, THE POOR LANDLORD WAS ALMOST CRYING BY THE TIME THAT I FINISHED MY GOOD EXPLANATION. HE KNEW THAT THE JUDGE WOULD SPARE US, AND THE JUDGE DID.

My father was a poor man, but he had not feared to speak in front of judges. Nor had he feared to speak in front of other groups, even his church: *HELP! MY PEOPLE ARE DYING! THEY NEED PRAYER! THEY NEED FOOD! THEY NEED BOOKS SO THAT THEY CAN LEARN!*

HELP! MY GRANDSON IN TIGRAY HAS NO PARENTS. HIS MOTHER, MY DAUGHTER, HAS DIED. HIS FATHER WAS A DERGUE SOLDIER WHO RAPED HIS MOTHER. PLEASE HELP HIM.

Most Americans would have dismissed a poor, handicapped refugee like my father, but the beautiful folks at Wheaton Bible Church remained true to their calling.

They saw past his disguise, and they helped him the best that they could, even sending monthly checks to his orphaned grandson.

I wonder sometimes if God sent my father to test the truest sentiments of their hearts. I wonder if God sends angels to all of us.

My father was never afraid to ask for help. But he also used his own power to help others, especially the most recently arrived refugees. The poorer the refugees, and the more desperately they needed his help, the more he wanted to do for them.

The most desperate families usually came with five or six children, and with parents too old to understand life in the States. Landlords in Wheaton rarely rented to them.

There was one exception: a landlord who rented out his basement. The families would pile in like sardines, up to 10 people huddled in three dark rooms. Somalis, Eritreans, Ethiopians, Kenyans, Cambodians—they all moved in, one family after the other.

Since my father knew Arabic, Tigrynia, Amharic, Giiz, English, and even a little Italian, he could usually communicate with the families, even with the non-*habesha*.

Sometimes he would take a detour before he visited them, walking to the grocery store to buy bread and fruit.

He would carry the bread and fruit to the cellar dwellers and talk with the parents and the kids. He would encourage the kids to educate themselves, and the parents to discipline their kids: *IF YOU LOVE YOUR CHILDREN AND WANT THEM TO BECOME GOOD PEOPLE, YOU MUST DISCIPLINE THEM NOW, BEFORE IT IS TOO LATE.*

On many occasions, he translated for the parents at Public Aid or at school. Other times, he introduced them to extra sources of funding. He helped so much that World Relief Refugee Services eventually gave him a special certificate in recognition of his tireless dedication.

We watched in wonder as he showed us this badge of honor, as he framed it and kept it near him. We asked ourselves, how could this simple piece of paper inspire such joy and happiness in him? How could it make him radiate so?

Maybe the answer lay in his past, and in the greatness he had known as an advanced dresser of wounds who could help others in their time of need.

Life as a beetle had often cloaked it, but that same source of greatness still pulsated here in the States. That greatness continues to pulsate—if not in my father, then in those he helped and the stories they still tell about him:

"When I found out that my mother had died back in Adi, Father Haileab came over and stayed with me for three days, never leaving my side, asking me what he could get for me, how he could support me."

"When I found out that my 13-year-old daughter was pregnant and the father unknown, Father Haileab came and wept with me, and counseled me, praying for my daughter and me for hours, encouraging both of us to keep our hopes burning."

"When my son graduated from college, Father Haileab came to my home, bearing gifts, and hugged me, and laughed with me, and danced with me for hours on end."

"When I first came to this country and I knew no one, Father Haileab let me stay in his home so that I would not have to live in the motel, and he even went with me to the Public Aid center, and stood in line with me for hours, and helped translate and advocate for me."

"When the policemen threw me into the house of imprisonment, Father Haileab collected $20 from each habesha family and begged a ride to the station to free me."

"When a car broke my leg in two and I had to sleep in the hospital for two days, Father Haileab sat up with me and then even came home with me."

"When my son had no place to stay, and I had nowhere to go, Father Haileab risked the wrath of Public Aid and hid my son in his home for several months."

I do not remember much of what was said during his funeral, for I am not good at remembering such things. The little I remember was said in the language he loved and fought for, his native Tigrynia:

Haileab lowha, ruruh, fetawee dikha, mejemera ni himoom kihiigeez, meewadaata kigedfoam, fetahwee hizboo, abona, keydu alo, ata zelalem, hijee nisilee kitkibolo.

Haileab the kindhearted, the compassionate, friend to the poor and the downtrodden, the first to comfort the sick, the last to leave them, ally of his people, our father and shepherd, he has gone up, and we pray, oh, Eternal One, that you receive him.

Oh, that he would have been here in the flesh to hear it.

Izgihare Yihabkoom

Sometimes I wonder what my father would have done at my graduation from Harvard. He probably would have leaped up from his seat and interrupted my commencement speech in front of 30,000 spectators. Standing with his back straight, chest out, and right hand pointing forward, he would have shouted, loud enough for everyone to hear:

THIS IS MY SON, SELAMAWI. A LONG TIME AGO, WHEN HE WAS JUST A LITTLE ONE, I TAUGHT HIM TO WORK HARD AND TO RESPECT OTHERS. NOW LOOK WHERE THAT HAS TAKEN HIM.

To my speech coach's dismay, I might have bowed and shouted back: "This is my father, Haileab. The woman next to him, with her quivering hands raised to the heavens, is my mother, Tsege. And I'm proud of both of them, too."

But like my brother, my father missed my graduation. Another drunk driver killed him during my junior year at Harvard.

Ironic, isn't it, that father and son survived disease, war and famine in Africa, but could not survive something as preventable as drinking and driving in America?

My father departed before it came to full fruition, but the dream that he and my mother shared has already begun to come true. His children have graduated from college—

first me, then Mehret, and one day, Hntsa. Mulu lives in Atlanta and raises two more children with that same dream.

I graduated from Harvard one year ago and have since thought much about my parents' dream. By earning my scholarship and graduating, I have fulfilled it.

But along the way, I have found greater value in other dreams. And while Harvard University taught me well, my true education has come from less-likely sources. As I look back to the angels, the Charlenes and the Beth Raneys; as I look back to God's servants, dressed as beggars and as beetles; as I look back to my inspirations, to the Mamas and Tewoldes, I see true guidance staring back at me.

True power comes from focusing on what we can give, not just on what we can take.

Of the gifts that we can give, the greatest is to see beauty in each other—in essence, to give beauty to each other. When we give that beauty, we prepare our hearts to receive it back.

So it is that I have been inspired by beetles and angels.

So it is that I hope you will be, too. When you are, I hope that you will remember this story about an immigrant's dream. As long as you remember, you'll share the spirit of the two who dreamed it.

As they say among my people, *Izgihare Yihabkoom.*

May God give to you.

Acknowledgements

The great Professor Cornel West once wrote, "We are who we are because someone loved us, cared for us and believed in us...."

To my boy Mike, for his great heart, for all the support that he has given me, and most of all, for being my boy.

To Ed Porter for encouraging me to start my speaking business, and to Corey McQuade for lending me the courage to make it full time.

To my friends Liz Drogin, Justin Porter, Alexander Band, Abby Fung, Jen Chau, Arden O'Connor, Asha Parekh, Aaron VanGetson, Rahwa Haile, Sewit Ahderom, Garrett Smith, and Getachew Kassa, thank you for your priceless help in editing this book. Special thanks to Amy Reynolds and Bo Menkiti for reading so many drafts so quickly.

To Ben Kaplan, author of *How to Go to College Almost for Free*, for your countless insights and enthusiastic support.

To all my pals at ShopTalk, for always rooting for me, and especially for supporting me financially and emotionally after the thief broke into my apartment.

To Harvard's model house tutor, Ben Berger, for always being in my corner, and always going to bat for me—you make the difference, Ben.

To Mrs. Benson, Viva Jones, and Myrtle Amundson, for being our American grandmothers.

To Shastine, a Swedish missionary who became a close friend to us in the camp, for coming across the world to visit us after we came to America, and for leaving the cover picture of Tewolde and Mehret—I hope that this book finds its way into your hands.

To Doug Portman, for taking such joy in my father,

To Linda Murphy and Peggy Coretti for taking such joy in my mother,

To the Linszs and Davidsons, for taking such joy in all of us.

To Charlie Trotter, for your boundless generosity, for allowing me to contribute to your culinary education program, and for finding time in your demanding schedule to review this book.

To Hayelom Ayele, for making time to review this book, for your many insights, for your good example, and for all the good work that you do on behalf of immigrants and refugees.

To Harry Lewis, for creating time to review this book, and for your fantastic feedback—the reader has you to thank for the chapter entitled, "Eyeing the Mountaintop."

To all the Wheaton North track coaches—Helberg, Eckman, Graf, McQuaid—and especially to Coach Martin, for giving me some of the best memories of my life and training me for the most important race of all.

To Susan Martin, for showing me boundless love, and for encouraging me to apply to and then attend Harvard.

To all the beautiful people in School District 200, everyone from Mrs. Mulholland and Mrs. Schaeffer in first grade, to the Lucketts, Dr. Langlas, Mr. Crowl and so many others in high school, and Denie Young after high school—you know I wouldn't be writing this without you.

To Ben Harper, for singing from your heart and inspiring mine—you set the bar just one notch higher, bro.

To a truly outstanding writer, and a great friend, my editor, Dave Berger. You have taken this book to a level that I never could have taken it to on my own. Special thanks.

To the wonderful folks at megadee books.

To my American mother, Candi Olander, who adopted me as one of her own, thank you for supporting me during my low times, having faith in me during my hard times, and loving me always.

To Harvard University, for the educations, for the friendships, and yes, even for the challenges. Thank you for investing in me.

To World Relief and Bethel Presbyterian Church, I ask, what thanks can I ever offer you, when you have given me a new lease on life?

To Wheaton Bible Church, and especially, the Couples for Christ fellowship, I do not have the words or power to thank you, you more than any other Americans have inspired and stunned and changed me through your love. I join my father and we yell out emphatically to the heavens: *"GOD BLESS WHEATON BIBLE CHURCH AND GOD BLESS COUPLES FOR CHRIST!"* You are easily known by your love.

To my people, my *habesha* brothers and sisters, both Eritreans and Ethiopians, all you who have been our family away from our family, and soothed our hearts when we most needed it, it lies not within human power to repay you—I can only pray that *amlahk baaloo yihabkoom*

To Mulu, Nega, Matthew, and Hannah, for all your love.

To you who I treasure more than anything in the world, my closest companions on this slow-swift adventure we call life, Mama, Mehret, and Hntsa. I hope that the preceding pages have done you right.

To my father, for your inner fire, for teaching us to see angels, and for your persistent faith that we could make it.

To you who meant more than life itself, for your love and faith, for all you have given and all you have inspired—*God be with us, and may we meet again.*

And finally to the spirit that has guided and watched me. I thank you for the life and breath you give me, and pray that you lead me in good paths, and give me the faith, hope, and love to move forward until that written day comes, journey ends, and you receive me back to your eternal fold.

The HAT Foundation

The HAT (Haileab And Tewolde) Foundation is a nonprofit organization with two missions:

1) To provide educational resources and emotional support for recently arrived third-world immigrants in the United States.

2) To provide funding for AIDS and malaria relief in Ethiopia and Eritrea.

The author is donating one-third of all proceeds from *Of Beetles and Angels* to The HAT Foundation.

Readers who wish to support The HAT Foundation can send contributions to:

MEGADEE BOOKS
Attn: The HAT Foundation
P.O. BOX 57060
Chicago, IL 60657-060

Praise for Mawi as a Speaker:

"Once in a while you hear someone that can change your thoughts, your attitude, and your life. Mawi Asgedom is one such person."
Swanton Enterprise, local paper, article written by two high school students: Aaron Redd and Kerry McQuade, 4/11/2000.

"The messages in a motivational speech given to the Wheaton North High School Freshman class Friday were likely old hat. Don't drink and drive. Success comes from taking risks. Believe in yourself.

"But those messages sank in because the messenger— Ethiopian refugee, former Wheaton North student, and Harvard graduate Mawi Asgedom—was like no one they'd ever seen before."
The Daily Herald, article written by David R. Kazak, staff writer, 11/1/1999.

"As coordinator of special programs at Steinmetz Academic Centre, I have coordinated many programs featuring motivational speakers for more than ten years. I consider Mawi among the very best."
Michael Altman, Special Programs Coordinator, Steinmetz Academic Centre, Chicago.

About the Author

Selamawi Asgedom fled war-torn Ethiopia at age three. For the next three years, he lived with his family in a Sudanese refugee camp.

He immigrated to the United States at age seven. Growing up, he overcame considerable language, cultural and financial challenges and eventually earned a full-tuition scholarship to Harvard University.

At Harvard, Asgedom won many top honors, including the Frothingham Prize: "Given each year to the member of the Senior Class at Harvard College, who in the opinions of the President of said Corporation, and the Deans of the College, best exemplifies the qualities of excellent scholarship, manliness, and effective support of the best interests of Harvard University."

He graduated as one of eight Class Marshals, and delivered the Commencement Address to over 30,000 people at his graduation in 1999.

Asgedom currently works full time as an inspirational speaker for students, community groups and businesses.

He lives in Chicago. He is twenty-four years old.